China Mission Studies (1550–1800) Bulletin
(as of vol. 11:)  Sino-Western Cultural Relations Journal
中西文化交流史雜誌（中國天主教史研究）1.1979–
38.2016
Edited and published by David E. Mungello

AF221444

# A Research Tool

## By Hartmut Walravens

BoD
2020

The cover illustration is taken from Wang Zhen & Johannes Schreck: *Yuanxi Qiqi tushuo* (ed. 1628, chapter III, plate 14). It shows the upper part of a windmill, after Fausto Veranzio: *Machinae novae*.

© 2020, by Hartmut Walravens
ISBN 978-3-7526-2887-6

Bibliografische Information der Deutschen Nationalbibliothek: Die Deutsche National-bibliothek verzeichnet diese Publikation in der Deutschen Nationalbibliografie; detaillierte bibliografische Daten sind im Internet über dnb.dnb.de abrufbar.
Herstellung und Verlag: BoD – Books on Demand, Norderstedt

David E. Mungello

# Preface

In the 1970s the study of Chinese history was in flux. The Cultural Revolution was reaching its destructive conclusion in the dismantling of the traditional Chinese cultural structure. Likewise, the study of the massive historical effort of Christian missionaries in China had become paralyzed by an apologetic tone. Into this vacuum came many new ideas for studying China. This thirst for new approaches became apparent in the surprising degree of interest in the publication of my revised dissertation *Leibniz and Confucianism: the Search for Accord*. It was published by the University of Hawaii Press (1977), one of the few research centers then devoted to East-West studies, as developed by the philosopher Charles Moore. Few historians, apart from outliers like Donald Lach who compiled the multi-volume *Asia in the Making of Europe* were then interested in what would come to be called Sino-Western history. In the 1960s the dominant view of China historians toward the study of the Christian missions in China was that it had become discredited by Western imperialism. Even Confucianism was regarded as archaic and of interest only as a vestige of the past. Unlike my professors at Berkeley and at most other major research universities, only isolated figures like John King Fairbank at Harvard were sympathetic to my suggestions for a new approach.

However, German scholarship was more sympathetic and the Alexander von Humboldt Stiftung supported my two years of research at the Leibniz Archiv in Hannover in 1978–1980. In 1984 the Herzog August Bibliothek in Wolfenbüttel sponsored a third year of research. The resulting manuscript was evaluated and rejected by several American university presses, including Princeton and Columbia, but was eventually published as *Curious Land: Jesuit Accommodation and the Origins of Sinology* in Germany in 1985 by the Steiner Verlag in the Studia Leibnitiana series. The book was widely reviewed and later reprinted in a paperback edition by the University of Hawaii Press. Its lasting significance was confirmed twenty-five years later when it was published in Chinese translation by a mainland Chinese press.

Initially I found a greater interest in new approaches to Sino-Western history among European scholars than among Americans. This interest led me to found a small journal initially called the *China Mission Studies (1550-1800) Bulletin* in West Germany in 1979. During the first ten years of its publication, a new field was coalescing which led, with the advice of Professor Fairbank, to the periodical's renaming as the *Sino-Western Cultural Relations Journal*. In an effort to involve Chinese scholars, the title was chosen as a translation of the Chinese phrase "Zhongxi wenhua jiaoliu shi zazhi" 中西文化交流史雜誌. After my return to the United States, North American interest in the *Journal* grew. It was always a shoe-string operation that depended on the willingness of scholars, notably Knud Lundbaek, Hartmut Walravens, Claudia von Collani, Ad Dudink, Nicolas Standaert, Eugenio Menegon, Gail King, Robert Entenmann, Walter Demel, Jonathan Chaves, Gad C. Isay, Theodore Nicholas Foss, Roman Malek, SVD, Matteo Nicolini-Zani, Mario Cams, Jocelyn M. N. Marinescu and Noël Golvers, to contribute articles, book reviews and necrologies. The SWCRJ was something of a "missionary" effort in that complimentary copies were sent to Chinese scholars in an attempt to stimulate genuine Sino-Western cultural exchange and foster a less-blatantly ideological form of scholarship in Sino-Western history than had marked the years under Mao Zedong. Several of these Chinese scholars, including Lin Jinshui 林金水, Hao Zhenhua 郝鎮華, Shen Dingping 沈定平, Han Qi 韓琦, Song Liming 宋黎明, and Wu Huiyi 吳蕙儀 became contributors. We were able to print most of the articles in the original language used by the authors (Chinese, French and German as well as English). The SWCRJ was produced annually for thirty-eight volumes until 2017 when it was forced to close due to the failure of my academic institution to provide the minimal support needed after my retirement from teaching. All back issues remain accessible through EBSCO Historical Abstracts with Full Text.

The SWCRJ began with an idea and a willingness of scholars to contribute to this venture. I typed the first issue on a manual typewriter in the Niedersächsische Landesbibliothek in Hannover and paid to have it photocopied. I collated it and mailed it out on a complimentary basis to elicit subscriptions. Over time, the subscriber list, although always small, contained some of the leading scholars in Sino-Western history and some of the most eminent research libraries in the world. It is a testament to what scholars can achieve together, without ever receiving a single financial grant from a foundation or government agency.

D. E. Mungello

# Contents

Preface by David E. Mungello ....................................................................... 5

Editor's notes ........................................................................................... 9

Bibliography .............................................................................................. 11

Index of personal names ........................................................................ 59

Subject index ........................................................................................... 67

# Editor's Notes

Though not belonging to the frequent contributors of SWCRJ I always liked to read it and keep up to date of the latest publications which often were reviewed. Nevertheless, I happened to be represented in the first and the last issue published, so I felt some personal attachment to it, and as I librarian I was aware of the need to make the cornucopia of information provided in this journal more easily available. That is how the present bibliography came into being.

It is now more than 40 years ago that David and I met briefly in Wolfenbüttel. There he persuaded me to contribute a note on Father Boym's *Flora sinensis* to the first issue of the journal; a more important result of this meeting was the exhibition *China illustrata* which David had conceived but could not, much to his regret, realize personally as his stay in Germany was coming to a close. So I took over, and the event (opened by the Chinese foreign minister) and the catalogue (enriched by an essay from David) became very successful.

*A few technical remarks on the present bibliography*
Chinese characters are presented in the traditional (long) form; in cases where the journal uses the simplified form it was converted to the long form.

In a number of cases Chinese titles are given only in Chinese script. Then a transliteration and translation were added in square brackets.

In the later editions of the journal authors names are accompanied by their Chinese equivalents; while these are usually reproduced when first cited, no efforts have been made to repeat them later on; they were entered in the index, however.
In many cases the metadata contain publishers information on the number of illustrations, tables, graphs, paper etc. These have not been copied because they are not particularly relevant for quoting or locating the respective information. Besides, Prof. Mungello was very careful in recording the ISBN by means of which the title records may be retrieved in many library and union catalogues so there would be no need of duplicating certain data.

In the tables of contents references are made to the issue, year of publication and the page numbers of the journal the name of which is not repeated.
Abbreviations of religious orders are given uniformly without dots, e.g. SJ, SVD.

The transliteration scheme changed over the years, from Wade/Giles to Pinyin. For the present bibliography Pinyin was chosen. When applicable, the Pinyin transliteration was added in square brackets.

# Bibliography

## 1.1979

1 The first translation from a Confucian Classic in Europe. By Knud Lundbæk.
   1.1979, 2–11
   [re: *Confucius Sinarum Philosophus.* Paris 1687.]

2 Notices sur l'histoire des missions de Chine (1552–1800) aux Archives des Jésuites de Paris.
   Par Joseph Dehergne SJ.
   1.1979, 12–15

3 News & notes of China Mission Studies (1550–1800).
   1.1979, 15

4 Eine Anmerkung zu Michael Boyms *Flora sinensis* (1656) – einer wichtigen
   naturhistorischen Quelle. Von Hartmut Walravens.
   1.1979, 16–20
   [Some notes on Boym's Flora sinensis and discussion of the description of the pineapple.]

5 Source materials for China Mission Studies (1550–1800). Report #1 The Chinese Collection
   at Berlin. By David E. Mungello.
   1.1979, 20–22

6 Supplement #2, China Mission Studies Directory.
   1.1979, 23
   [This refers to the *China Mission Studies Directory* which was published by the editor in New
   York 1978. 31 pp. The first supplement consisted of 3 columns, dated September 1978.]

## 2.1980

7 Note sur "L'explication générale de la géometrie" jihé tongjie (幾何通解) de Méi Wénding
   梅文鼎 (1633–1721). Par Jean Claude Martzloff.
   2.1980, 3–12

8 Report on the IIIe Colloque international de sinologie de Chantilly (September 11–14, 1980).
   By Edmund Leites.
   2.1980,13–14

9 Source materials for China Mission Studies (1550–1800). Report #2: The Chinese collection
   in the Biblioteca Apostolica Vaticana. By David E. Mungello.
   2.1980, 15–18

10 News & notes of China Mission Studies.
   2.1980, 19

11 Clarifying note from the editor [re Dehergne's article]. – Supplement # 3 China Mission
   Studies (1550–1800) Directory.
   2.1980, 19


### 3.1981

12 News of the field.
   3.1981, 1

13 Chief Grand Secretary Chang Chü-cheng [Zhang Juzheng] & the early China Jesuits. By
   Knud Lundbæk.
   3.1981, 2–11

14 The Jesuits' use of Chang Chü-cheng's [Zhang Juzheng] commentary in their translation of
   the Confucian Four Books (1687). By David E. Mungello.
   3.1981, 12–22

15 Source material for China Mission Studies  (1550–1800) #3: The Woodstock Theological
   Center Library, Georgetown University. By Ann Nottingham Kelsall.
   3.1981, 23–24


### 4.1982

16 The True Meaning of the Lord of Heaven (T'ien-chu Shih-i [*Tianzhu shiyi*]). By Matteo Ricci
   SJ. Translated, with notes, by Douglas Lancashire.
   4.1982, 1–11

17 Chinese figurism in the eyes of European contemporaries. By Claudia von Collani.
   4.1982, 12–23

18 Die Schrift T'ien-hsüeh ch'uan-kai 天學傳概 [*Tianxue chuangai*] als eine
   Zwischenformulierung der jesuitischen Anpassungsmethode im 17. Jahrhundert. Von David E.
   Mungello.
   4.1982, 24-39

19 Convegno internazionale su Martino Martini (Trento 1614–Hangzhou 1661): geografo,
   cartografo, storico, teologo, Trento, Italy, October 9–10th 1981. By Knud Lundbæk.
   4.1982, 39

20 Source materials for China Mission Studies (1550–1800). Report 4: The Leiden Sinological
   Institute Library, Leiden State University (The Netherlands). By Nicholas Standaert.
   4.1982, 40-44


### 5.1983

21 Ein neues Hilfsmittel beim Studium der christlichen chinesischen Literatur. Von H.
   Walravens.
   5.1983, 1–2

[Announces the publication of: *Preliminary checklist of Christian and western material in Chinese in three major collections. – Vorläufige Titelliste christlicher und westlicher Literatur in chinesischer Sprache in drei bedeutenden Sammlungen.* Hamburg: C. Bell 1983. II, 75 pp.]

22 East meets West: The Jesuits in China, 1582–1773. Conference at Loyola University, Chicago, October 7–9, 1982. By John W. Witek SJ.
5.1983, 3–4

23 Imaginary ancient Chinese characters. By Knud Lundbæk.
5.1983, 5–23
[An investigation of the strange Chinese characters printed by Athanasius Kircher in his *China illustrata*, 1667.]

24 Report on the Convegno internazionale di studi Ricciani nel IV centenario dell'arrivo in Cina di Matteo Ricci, SI. By Theodore Nicholas Foss.
5.1983, 24–27

25 A note on Jesuit works in Chinese which circulated in seventeenth- and eighteenth century Korea. By Donald L. Baker.
5.1983, 28–36

26 Library report 5: Sources for China Mission Studies (1550–1800) preserved in the Niedersächsische Staats- und Universitätsbibliothek Göttingen, Bundesrepublik Deutschland. By David E. Mungello.
5.1983, 37–43

27 News of the field.
5.1983, 44

28 Correction from the editor [re Bibliogr. no. 18].
5.1983, 44

**6.1984**

29 A survey of the Chinese intellectual's anti-Christian opinions as related to the cultural exchange between China and the West (1583–1723). By Lü Shih-chiang [Lü Shijiang 呂實強].
6.1984, 1–3

30 Lü Shih-chiang [Lü Shijiang] 呂實強: Yu Ming-Ch'ing chih chi Chung-kuo chih-shih fen-tzu fan-chiao yen-lun k'an Chung-hsi wen-hua chiao-liu (1583–1723).
由明清之際中國知識分子反教言論看中西文化交流 [You Ming Qing zhi ji zhongguo zhishi fenzi fanjiao yanlun kan zhongxi wenhua jiaoliu].
6.1984, 4–42

31 Présentation de la première trigonométrie chinoise, le *Dace* 大測 / Bai Shangshu 白尚恕
   (Academia Sinica, Pékin).
   6.1984, 43–50

32 The Matteo Ricci quadricentennial celebration in the Philippines: The true humanist becomes
   a bridge between civilizations. Manila, August–September 1983.
   6.1984, 51–52
   This report represents a condensation of material kindly provided by Fr. I. Zuloaga SJ.

33 Hong Kong celebrates Matteo Ricci anniversary, September 11th 1983. By the Rev. Elmer P.
   Wurth, MM.
   6.1984, 52–53

34 Commemorative stamps issued [Taiwan].
   6.1984, 53

35 Matteo Ricci's legacy in East Asia. A conference at Sogang University, Seoul, Korea,
   October 21–22, 1983. By Donald L. Baker.
   6.1984, 54–55

36 Rapport sur le IVème Colloque international de sinologie, Chantilly 1983. Par Egly
   Alexandre.
   6.1984, 56–57

37 Francis A. Rouleau, SJ. (1900–1984).
   6.1984, 58–59
   Theodore N. Foss, Edward J. Malatesta

38 Publication notes from the field.
   6.1984, 60

39 Correction from the editor [re Lundbæk article, no. 23].
   6.1984, 60

## 7.1985

40 Matteo Ricci in the *Aomen jilüe* 澳門記略. By Knud Lundbæk.
   7.1985, 2–13

41 Lin Chin-shui [Lin Jinshui] 林金水: Ju-chiao pu shih tsung-chiao 儒教不是宗教 [Rujiao
   bushi zongjiao][Is Confucianism a religion？ An attempt to present the viewpoint of Matteo
   Ricci toward Confucianism].
   7.1985, 14–21
   Aus Fu-chien shih-ta hsüeh-pao [*Fujian shida xuebao*] 1983, Nr 3

42 Note on the spread of Jesuit writings in late Ming and early Qing China. By Nicholas
   Standaert.
   7.1985, 22–32

New publications in the field

43 [rev.] T. S. Bayer (1694–1738): Pioneer sinologist. By Knud Lundbæk. London: Curzon Press 1985. 305 pp. (Scandinavian Institute of Asian Studies 54.)
7.1985, 33

44 [rev.] Curious land: Jesuit accomodation & the origins of sinology by David E. Mungello. Wiesbaden: Steiner 1985. 405 pp. (Studia Leibnitiana. Supplement 25.)
7.1985, 33–34

45 [rev.] Christian Wolff: Rede über die praktische Philosophie der Chinesen (Oratio de Sinarum philosophia practica). Lateinisch-deutsch. Übersetzt und mit einer Einleitung herausgegeben von Michael Albrecht. Hamburg: Felix Meiner 1985. 324 pp. (Philosophische Bibliothek 374.)
7.1985, 35

46 [rev.] Scholars' guide to China mission resources in the libraries and archives of the United States (Pennsylvania fascicle) by Archie R. Crouch. Princeton University Press 1983. 84 pp.
7.1985, 36

## 8.1986

47 Wang Qingyu 王慶余: Li Madou xiewu kao 利瑪竇携物考. [A guide to investigating Matteo Ricci.]
8.1986, 2–40
[This article is reprinted from the inaugural issue of the periodical *Zhongwai guanxishi luncong* 中外關係史論叢 (Collected essays on the history of Sino-foreign relations) 1.1985, 78–116.]

48 The Xujiahui (Zikawei) Library of Shanghai in 1986. By D. E. Mungello.
8.1986, 41–56

49 The Institute for Chinese-Western Cultural History (San Francisco).
8.1986, 57–58

50 Ricci Institute for Chinese Studies, Taipei.
8.1986, 59–60

Publications in the field:

51 [rev.] P. Joachim Bouvet S. J., sein Leben und sein Werk. Von Claudia von Collani. Nettetal: Steyler Verlag 1985. XII, 296 pp. (Monumenta serica monograph series 17.)
8.1986, 61–62

52 [rev.] The True Meaning of the Lord of Heaven (T'ien-chu shih-i 天主實義 [*Tianzhu shiyi*]) by Matteo Ricci, SJ. Translated with introduction and notes, by Douglas Lancashire and Peter Hu Kuo-chen SJ. A Chinese-English edition, edited by Edward J. Malatesta SJ. St. Louis: Institute of Jesuit Sources, Taipei: Ricci Institute 1985. XIV, 485 pp. (Variétés sinologiques N.S. 72.)
8.1986, 62–63

53 [rev.] Jesuit and friar in the Spanish expansion to the East, by J. S. Cummins. London:
   Variorum 1986. 334 pp., 2 Kt.
   8.1986, 63–64

54 [rev.] A. C. Moule 阿克穆尔著: Yiwu wu ling nianqiandi Zhongguo jidujiao shi
   一五五〇年前的中國基都教史 [Christians in China before the year 1550]. Hao Zhenhua yi
   郝鎮華譯 [translated by Hao Zhenhua]. Beijing: Zhonghua shuju 1984.
   8.1986, 64

55 [Philippe] Couplet Symposium at Leuven, September 1986.
   8.1986, 65

56 Vème Colloque international de sinologie de Chantilly (1986).
   8.1986, 66–67

**9.1987**

57 Lin Jinshui 林金水: Li Madou jiaoyou renwu biao 利瑪竇交游人物表. [A list of Matteo
   Ricci's friendships with eminent figures.]
   9.1987, 1–27
   [Reprinted from *Zhongwai guanxishi luncong* 1.1985, 117–143.]

58 Ein figuristisches Spätwerk Joachim Bouvets. Von Claudia von Collani.
   9.1987, 28–37

59 The Jesuits' preaching of the Buddha in China. By Nicholas Standaert.
   9.1987, 38–41

60 China and Europe: 16th–18th centuries – Symposium.
   9.1987, 41–43
   D. E. M.

   New publications in the field:
61 [rev.] Das vergessene Gedächtnis. Die jesuitische mnemotechnische Abhandlung *Xiguo jifa*.
   Übersetzung und Kommentar. Von Michael Lackner. Stuttgart: Franz Steiner 1986. X, 139 pp.
   (Münchener Ostasiatische Studien 42.)
   9.1987, 44–45

62 [rev.] Confucius, the Buddha and Christ: A history of the gospel in Chinese, by Ralph R.
   Covell. Maryknoll, N.Y.: Orbis Books 1986.
   9.1987, 45–46

63 [rev.] Li Madou Zhongguo zhaji 利瑪竇中國札記 [Ricci's *Historia* manuscript], transl. He
   Gaoji 何高濟, Wang Zunzhong 王遵仲, Li Shen 李申. Peking: Zhonghua shuju 1983. 705 pp.
   9.1987, 46

64 [rev.] Xu Guangqi ji 徐光啓集 [Collection of works by Xu Guangqi], ed. by Wang Zhongmin 王重民輯校.
Shanghai: Guji chubanshe 1984. 50, 641 pp.
9.1987, 47

65 [rev.] Zhongxi jiaotong shi 中西交通史 [A history of Sino-Western contacts]. Fang Hao zhu 方豪著.
Taibei: Zhongguo wenhua daxue chubanbu 1983. (Reprint of the 1953 edition). 27, 1075 pp.
9.1987, 47

66 [rev.] Zhongxi wenhua jiaoliu shi 中西文化交流史 [A history of Sino-Western cultural interchange]. Shen Fuwei zhu 沈福偉著.
Shanghai: Renmin chubanshe 1984. 9, 469 pp.
9.1987, 48

## 10.1988

67 A note to the reader: tenth anniversary issue.
10.1988, 1–2
D. E. Mungello, editor

68 [Shen Dingping: Zhongguo gudai sixiang dui xi'ou qimeng yundong di yingxiang]
沈定平：中國古代思想對歐啟蒙運動旳影响 [The influence of ancient Chinese thought upon the Enlightenment movement of Western Europa].
10.1988, 3–8
[Originally appeared in *Wenshi zhishi* 文史知識 1.1986, 59–64]

69 *Tianxue benyi* – Joachim Bouvets Forschungen zum Monotheismus. Von Claudia von Collani.
10.1988, 9–33
[*Tianxue benyi* 天學本義]

70 Unearthing the manuscripts of Bouvet's *Gujin* after nearly three centuries. By D. E. Mungello.
10.1988, 34–61
[*Gujin jing tian Tianxue benyi* 古今敬天鑒天學本義]

71 News & notes of the field.
10.1988, 62–63

72 [rev.] K'ung-tzu or Confucius? The Jesuit interpretation of Confucius by Paul A. Rule.
Sydney, London, Boston: Allen & Unwin 1986. XIII, 303 pp. ISBN 08-86861-9132
10.1988, 64–66
D. E. M.

73 [rev.] China illustrata. Das europäische Chinaverständnis im Spiegel des 16. bis 18. Jahrhunderts. Ausstellungskatalog der Herzog August Bibliothek vom 21. März bis 23. August 1987. Ausstellung und Katalog von Hartmut Walravens mit einem Beitrag von David E. Mungello. Weinheim: Acta Humaniora 1987. 302 pp. ISBN 3-527-17815-5
10.1988, 66
D. E. M.

74 [rev.] A traditional history of the Chinese script. The seventeen unprinted pages from the manuscript of *Confucius Sinarum Philosophus*. Facsimile edition with translation and commentary by Knud Lundbæk. Aarhus: Aarhus University Press 1988. 64 pp. 4°
10.1988, 67
K. L[undbæk]

75 [rev.] [Xu Guangqi zhuyi ji] 徐光啟著譯集. Shanghai: Guji chubanshe 1983. 2 tao, 20 fascicles.
10.1988, 68
G. K.

76 [rev.] Michał Boym Ostatni wysłannik dynastii Ming (Michael Boym. The last envoy of the Ming Dynasty). By Edward Kajdański. Warsaw: Wydawnictwo Polonia 1988. 173 pp. ISBN 83-7021-021-X
10.1988, 69–71
E. K[ajdański]

77 [rev.] China illustrata by Athanasius Kircher SJ. Translated by Dr. Charles D. van Tuyl from the 1677 [i.e. 1667] original Latin edition. Muskogee: Indian University Press 1987. X, 228 pp.
10.1988, 71–72
D. E. M.

## 11.1989

78 [Xu Mingde: Shiqi shiji Yidali Hanxuejia Wei Kuangguo mudi kao]
徐明德：十七世紀義大利漢學家衛匡國墓地考 [On the tomb of the Italian Sinologist of the 17th century, Martin(o) Martini].
11.1989, 1–10

79 International Conference on the Life and Work of Ferdinand Verbiest in commemoration of the 300th anniversary of his death.
11.1989, 11–13
Knud Lundbæk

80 European-American Conference on Exchanges in East Asian Studies (1988).
11.1989, 13

81 Conference on the Encounter of Religions in China.
11.1989, 14

82 A search for Andreas Müller's Chinese manuscripts in Poland. By Edward Kajdański.
11.1989, 15–27
[Müller was the (honorary) Chinese Librarian to the Great Elector of Brandenburg.]

83 Abundantia, Sapientia, Decadencia – zum Wandel des Chinabildes vom 16. bis zum 18. Jahrhundert. Von Walter Demel.
11.1989, 28–37

84 [rev.] East meets West: The Jesuits in China, 1582–1773. Edited by Charles E. Ronan SJ and Bonnie B. C. Oh. Chicago: Loyola University Press 1988, XXXIII, 332 pp.
11.1989, 38–41
Min-sun Chen [Lakehead University, Thunder Bay, Ontario]

85 [rev.] Yang Tingyun, Confucian and Christian in late Ming China. His life and thought by N. Standaert. Leiden: E. J. Brill 1988. XI, 263 pp. (Sinica Leidensia 19.)
11.1989, 42–44
D. E. M.

86 [rev.] Vorschlag einer wissenschaftlichen Akademie für China. Briefe des Chinamissionars Joachim Bouvet SJ an Gottfried Wilhelm Leibniz und an den Präsidenten der Académie des Sciences Jean-Paul Bignon aus dem Jahre 1704 über die Erforschung der chinesischen Kultur, Sprache und Geschichte. Herausgegeben und kommentiert von Claudia von Collani. Stuttgart: Franz Steiner 1989. 136 pp. (Studia Leibnitiana. Sonderheft 18.)
11.1989, 44–45
D. E. M.

87 [rev.] Katalog der chinesischen und mandjurischen Bücher der Bibliothek der Akademie der Wissenschaften in St. Petersburg von Julius von Klaproth. Hrsg. v. H. Walravens. Berlin: Bell 1988. V, 45 pp. ISBN 3-923308-60-4
11.1989, 45–46
D. E. M.

88 [rev.] [John Lust:] Western books on China published up to 1850 in the Library of the School of Oriental and African Studies, University of London. A descriptive catalogue. London: Bamboo Publishing 1987. XII, 340 pp. ISBN 1-870076-02-8
11.1989, 46
D. E. M.

**12.1990**

89 Necrology: Joseph Dehergne SJ (1903–1990).
12.1990, 1–2
Edward Malatesta SJ, Institute for Chinese-Western Cultural History, Center for the Pacific Rim, University of San Francisco.

90 Preliminary bibliography of works by Joseph Dehergne SJ. Compiled by Theodore N. Foss, Stanford University.
12.1990, 3–6

91 Necrology: Joseph S. Sebes SJ (1915–1990).
12.1990, 7–9
John W. Witek SJ, Georgetown University

92 [Li Lanqin: *Tang Ruowang jianlun*] 李蘭琴：湯若望簡論. [Short essay on Fr. Schall von Bell SJ.]
12.1990, 10–28

93 Some new dimensions in the study of the works of James Legge (1815–1897). Part 1. By Lauren F. Pfister.
   12.1990, 29–50

94 VIe Colloque International de Sinologie. Chantilly, 11–14 Septembre 1989.
   12.1990, 51–53
   John W. Witek SJ, Georgetown University

95 History of Christianity in China project concludes.
   12.1990, 53–54
   D. E. M.

96 [rev.] The question of Hu. By Jonathan Spence. New York: Vintage Books 1989. XX, 187 pp. ISBN 0-679-72580-6
   12.1990, 55–56
   Knud Lundbæk, Aarhus University

97 [rev.] Christianity in China. A scholar's guide to resources in the libraries and archives of the United States. By Archie R. Crouch et al. Armonk, NY: M. E. Sharpe 1989. LVI,709 pp. ISBN 0-87332-419-6
   12.1990, 56–57
   D. E. M.

98 [rev.] Chinese hells. The Peking Temple of Eighteen Hells and Chinese conceptions of hell. By Anne Swann Goodrich. St. Augustin: Monumenta Serica 1981. III, 167 S, 32 Taf. 2nd printing 1989.
   12.1990, 58
   D. E. M.

99 Announcements.
   In memoriam Fr. J. Spae (1913–1989).
   12.1990, 59
   D. E. M.

100 List of contributors.
   12.1990, 60

## 13.1991

101 Liu Ning (Erzhi) 劉凝 （二至） [ca. 1658–1738]. A Chinese Christian author of the 17th–18th century. By Knud Lundbæk.
   13.1991, 1–3

102 The Jesuit presence in China (1580–1773). A statistical approach. By Nicolas Standaert SJ.
   13.1991, 4–17

103 [Hao Zhenhua: Lang Shining Zhongguo xiyu zhantu di shishi ji yiyi]
   郝鎮華：郎世寧中國西域戰圖旳史實及意義. [The historical facts and the significance of Castiglione's battle pictures of the Western Regions.]
   13.1991, 18–32
   [This article appeared originally in Meishu shilun 美術史論 3.1989.]

104 Some new dimensions in the study of the works of James Legge (1815–1897). Part 2. By Lauren F. Pfister.
13.1991, 33–48

105 Colloquium. – In memoriam [Giorgio Melis †1990].
13.1991, 48
D. E. M.

106 [rev.] Coming out of the Middle Ages. Comparative reflexions on China and the West. By Zhu Weizheng. Translated and edited by Ruth Hayhoe. Armonk, NY: M. E. Sharpe 1991. 225 pp. ISBN 0-87332-638-55
13.1991, 49–50
Thomas H. C. Lee, The City College, CUNY

107 [rev.] Philippe Couplet SJ (1623–1693): The man who brought China to Europe. Ed. by Jerome Heyndrickx. Louvain: Ferdinand Verbiest Foundation; Nettetal: Steyler Verlag 1990. 260 pp., 6 pl. (Monumenta serica monograph series 22.) ISBN 3-8050-0266-1
13.1991, 51–53
Min-sun Chen, Lakehead University, Thunder Bay, Ontario

108 [rev.] Leibniz korrespondiert mit China. Der Briefwechsel des Gottfried Wilhelm Leibniz mit Chinamissionaren, 1689–1714. Edited by Rita Widmaier. Frankfurt a.M.: Klostermann 1990. XVI, 332 pp.
13.1991, 53–54
D. E. M.

109 [rev.] Only the beginning. The Passionists in China, 1921–1931. By Caspar Caulfield CP. Union City, NJ: Passionist Press 1990. XV, 296 pp. ISBN 0-96261-190-5
13.1991, 54–55
D. E. M.

110 [rev.] Rawlinson, the *Recorder* and China's revolution. A topical biography of Frank Joseph Rawlinson 1871–1937. By John Lang Rawlinson. Notre Dame 1990. XII, 789 pp. ISBN 0-940121-12-3
13.1991, 55
D. E. M.

## 14.1992

111 [Lin Jinshui: Shilun Nan Huairen dui Kangxi tianzhujiao zhengce di yinxiang] 林金水：試論南懷仁對康熙天主教政策旳影响 [An examination of the influence of F. Verbiest on the policies of the Kangxi Emperor toward the Catholic Church.]
14.1992, 1–21
[Reprinted from *Shijie zongjiao yanjiu* 世界宗教研究 1991:1, pp. 54–67.]

112 Zwei Briefe zu den figuristischen Schriften Joachim Bouvets SJ. Von Claudia von Collani.
14.1992, 22–38

113 [rev.] Bibliography of the Jesuit mission in China, ca. 1580–ca. 1680. By Erik Zürcher, Nicolas Standaert SJ and Adrianus Dudink. Leiden: Centre of Non-Western Studies 1991. 136 pp. ISBN 90-73782-05-8

14.1992, 39–43
Lionel M. Jensen, Department of History, University of Colorado at Denver


114 [rev.] Bouddhisme, christianisme et société chinoise. By E. Zürcher. Introduction by Jacques
    Gernet. Paris: Julliard 1990. 95 pp. ISBN 2-260-00683-3
    14.1992, 43–44
    D. E. M.


115 [rev.] China and Europe, images and influences in sixteenth to eighteenth centuries. Edited by
    Thomas H. C. Lee. Hong Kong: The Chinese University Press 1991. VIII, 356 pp. ISBN 962-
    201-465-8
    14.1992, 45–46
    John D. Young, Honorary Research Fellow, Centre for Asian Studies, University of Hong
    Kong


116 [rev.] Dall'Europa alla Cina. Contributi per una storia dell'astronomia. Edited by Isaia
    Iannaccone and Adolfo Tamburello. Napoli: Università degli Studi "Federico II"; Istituto
    Orientale 1990. VII, 256 pp.
    14.1992, 47–48
    Giuliano Bertuccioli, Dipartimento degli studi orientali, Università di Roma I


117 [rev.] Discours sur la théologie naturelle des Chinois plus quelques écrits sur la question
    religieuse de Chine by G. W. Leibniz. Presented, translated and annotated by Christiane
    Frémont. Paris: L'Herne 1987. 217 pp. ISBN 2-85197-606-0
    14.1992, 48–50
    D. E. M.


118 [rev.] L'Europe chinoise. By R. Etiemble. I: De l'empire romain à Leibniz. Paris: Éditions
    Gallimard 1988. 438 pp. ISBN 2-07-071206-0 II: Sinophilie à le sinophobie. 1989. 399 pp.
    ISBN 2-07-071615-5
    14.1992, 50–52
    D. E. M.


119 [rev.] Johann Adam Schall von Bell SJ, Missionar in China, kaiserlicher Astronom und
    Ratgeber am Hofe von Peking 1592–1666. Ein Lebens- und Zeitbild by Alfons Väth SJ.
    Unter Mitwirkung von Louis van Hée SJ. Neue Auflage. Nettetal: Steyler Verlag 1991.
    XX,423 pp. (Monumenta serica monograph series 25.) ISBN 3-8050-0287-4
    14.1992, 52–53
    D. E. M.


120 [rev.] Joseph de Prémare (1666–1736) SJ. Chinese philology and figurism by Knud Lundbæk.
    Aarhus: Aarhus University Press 1991. 228 pp. (Acta Jutlandica 66,2.) ISBN 87-7288-344-8
    14.1992, 54–57
    Michael Lackner, Berlin


121 [rev.] Travels to real and imaginary lands. By Giuliano Bertuccioli. Edited with an appendix
    „Francesco Carletti on slavery and oppression" by Antonino Forte. Kyoto: Italian School of
    East Asian Studies 1990. VII, 85 pp. (Occasional Papers 2.)
    14.1992, 57–58
    D. E. M.

122 Symposium: J. A. Schall von Bell SJ, missionary of Cologne & astronomer of China.
14.1992, 59–61
Claudia von Collani, Würzburg

123 A note on the 300th anniversary of the Kangxi emperor's edict of toleration (1692).
14.1992, 62–63
C. von Collani, Würzburg

124 News of the field.
14.1992, 64


**15.1993**

125 The rediscovery of a seventeenth-century collection of Chinese Christian texts: The manuscripts *Tianxue jijie* [天學集解]. By Adrian Dudink.
15.1993, 1–26
[The texts were acquired by the Imperial Public Library in St. Petersburg in 1827.]

126 A different country, the same heaven. A preliminary biography of Giulio Aleni SJ (1582–1649). By Eugenio Menegon.
15.1993, 27–51

127 Pierre Martial Cibot (1727–1780) – the last China figurist. By Knud Lundbæk.
15.1993, 52–59

128 Necrology: Antonio Sisto Rosso OFM (1904–1990).
15.1993, 60–61
Bernward H. Willeke OFM

129 In memoriam [Fortunato Margiotti OFM, 1913–1990]
15.1993, 61
D. E. M.

130 In memoriam [Caspar Caulfield CP, †1993].
15.1993, 62
D. E. M.

131 [rev.] Buddhistische Kritik am Christentum im China des 17. Jahrhunderts. Texte von Yu Shunxi (?–1621), Zhuhong (1535–1615), Yuanwu (1566–1642), Tongrong (1593–1679), Xingyuan (1611–1662), Zhixu (1599–1655). Von Iso Kern. Bern: Peter Lang 1992. XIV, 418 pp. (Schweizer Asiatische Studien. Monographien 11.)
15.1993,63–65
D. E. M.

132 [rev.] Moral enlightenment: Leibniz and Wolff on China. By Julia Ching & Willard G. Oxtoby. Nettetal: Steyler Verlag 1992. XIII, 288 pp. (Monumenta serica monograph series 26.) ISBN 3-8050-0294-7
15.1993, 65–68
D. E. M.

133 [rev.] Als Fremde in China. Das Reich der Mitte im Spiegel frühneuzeitlicher europäischer
Reiseberichte. Von Walter Demel. München: R. Oldenbourg 1992. XXI, 329 pp.
15.1993, 68–69
D. E. M.

134 Some publications on late Ming – early Qing cultural exchange between East and West by
Mainland China authors.
15.1993, 70–74
Nicolas Standaert SJ
[On Sun Jiang 孫江: Shizijia yu long [The cross and the dragon]. Hangzhou 1990. 246 pp.,
Sun Shangyang 孫尚楊: Mingmo tianzhujiao yu ruxue de jiaoliu he chongtu [Exchange and
conflict between Catholicism and Confucianism in the late Ming period.]. Taibei 1992. 259
pp.; Chen Weiping 陳衛平: Diyiye yu peitai: Ming Qing zhi ji de zhongxi wenhua bijiao [The
first page and embryo. A comparison between Eastern and Western cultures in the transition
period of Ming and Qing]. Shanghai 1992. 281 pp.]

135 Symposium: The significance of the Chinese rites controversy in Sino-Western history.
15.1993, 75–76
D. E. M.

135a  Convegno Internazionale Giulio Aleni.
15.1993, 76


**16.1994**


136 [Huang Yinong: Cong "Shixinlu xu" xijiu Yang Guangxian di xingge] 黃一農：
從始信錄序析究楊光先旳性格 [Explaining Yang Guangxian's temperament drawing from
the *Shixinlu* preface.]
16.1994, 1–18

137 A previously unknown preface (1607) by Zhou Xianchen 周獻臣 to Ricci's *Tianzhu shiyi* 天
主實義. By Adrian Dudink.
16.1994, 19–36

138 Der deutsche Philosoph Gottfried Wilhelm Leibniz zum chinesischen Ritenstreit. Von
Claudia von Collani.
16.1994, 37–48

139 [rev.] Singing of the source: Nature and god in the poetry of the Chinese painter Wu Li. By
Jonathan Chaves. Honolulu: University of Hawaii Press 1993.) XIII, 208 pp (SHAPS Library
of Translations.) ISBN 0-8248-1485-1
16.1994, 49–54
Anthony C. Yu, University of Chicago

140 [rev.] A question of rites: Friar Domingo Navarrete and the Jesuits in China. By J. S.
Cummins. London: Scolar Press 1993. XV. 349 pp.
16.1994, 55–56
John E. Wills, jr., University of Southern California

141 [rev.] The *Astronomia europaea* of Ferdinand Verbiest S.J. (Dillingen, 1687). Text, translation, notes by Noel Golvers. Nettetal: Steyler Verlag 1993. 547 pp. (Monumenta serica monograph series 28.)
16.1994, 56–58
D. E. M.

142 [rev.] L'Europe en Chine. Interactions scientifiques, religieuses et culturelles aux XVIIe et XVIIIe siècles revus et établis par Catherine Jami et Hubert Delahaye. Actes du colloque de la Fondation Hugot (14–17 octobre 1991). Paris: De Boccard 1993. XIII, 255 pp. (Mémoires de l'Institut des Hautes Études Chinoises 34.) ISBN 2-85757-049-X
16.1994, 58–60
D. E. M.

143 [rev.] Asia in the making of Europe. Vol. 3: A century of advance. Book 1. Trade, missions, literature; Book 2. South Asia; Book 3. Southeast Asia; Book 4. East Asia. By Donald F. Lach and Edwin J. Van Kley. Chicago: University of Chicago Press 1993. LXXVI, 597; LVII, 601–1110; LIII, 1111–1561; CXII, 1563–2077
16.1994, 60–65
Lionel M. Jensen, Department of History, University of Colorado at Denver

144 [rev.] Die *Geschichte der höchst bemerkenswerten Dinge und Sitten im chinesischen Königreich* des Juan Gonzalez de Mendoza. Ein Beitrag zur Kulturgeschichte des ming-zeitlichen China, hrsg. v. Margareta Grießler. Sigmaringen: Jan Thorbecke 1992. 129 pp. ISBN 3-7995-7112-4
16.1994, 66–67
Walter Demel, München

145 [rev.] The forgotten Christians of Hangzhou. By D. E. Mungello. Honolulu: University of Hawaii Press 1994. XII, 248 pp. ISBN 0-8248-1540-8
16.1994, 67–69
John Dragon Young, Centre of Asian Studies, University of Hong Kong

146 [rev.] One hundred Roman documents concerning the Chinese Rites Controversy (1645–1941). Translations by Donald F. St. Sure SJ. Edited with introductions and summaries by Ray R. Noll. San Francisco: Ricci Institute 1992. XIX, 93 pp. (Studies in Chinese-Western Cultural History 1.)
16.1994, 70
D. E. M.

147 [rev.] Shanghai Library Catalog of Western Rare Books. Compiled as a joint effort of the Shanghai Library and the Ricci Institute for Chinese-Western Cultural History. With an introduction by Zhu Qingzuo. Shanghai: The Publishing House of the Shanghai Academy of Social Sciences 1992. XII,463 pp. ISBN 7-80515-776-6
16.1994, 71–72
D. E. M.

148 Archivo de la Provincia del Santo Rosario (APSR), formerly in the Convento de Santo Domingo, Manila, Philippines, now in the Convento de Santo Tomás (Real Monasterio), Avila, Spain. By Eugenio Menegon.
16.1994, 73–75

Symposia:
149 VIIe Colloque International de Sinologie.
16.1994, 76
Robert Entenmann, St. Olaf College

150 Symposium on Martin Martini SJ and Cultural Exchanges between China and the West (5–7 April 1994).
16.1994, 76–78
Claudia von Collani, Würzburg

151 News and notes of the field.
16.1994, 79

152 List of conributors.
16.1994, 80


**17.1995**

153 Necrology: Knud Lundbæk (1912–1995).
17.1995, 1–4
Claudia von Collani, Würzburg

154 Archivo Franciscano Ibero-Oriental (AFIO), Madrid (Spain).
17.1995, 4–5
Eugenio Menegon, Berkeley

155 The transformation of *Chinesia* from Jesuitical fiction to Jesuit college drama. A preliminary survey. By Adrian Hsia (McGill University, Montreal).
17.1995, 6–26

156 A brief note on the "rediscovery" of some French Jesuits' tombstones. By Giovanni Stary (University of Venice, Italy).
17.1995, 27–28

157 The treatise on Chinese religions (1623) of N. Longobardi SJ. By Claudia von Collani.
17.1995, 29–37

158 Etienne Fourmont (1683–1745): The birth of sinology in the context of the institutions of learning in eighteenth-century France. By Cécile Leung.
17.1995, 38–56

159 International Symposium "Giulio Aleni SJ (1582–1649), Missionary in China".
17.1995, 57–58
Eugenio Menegon, Berkeley

160 Simpósio internacional religião e cultura comemorativo Colégio Universitário de S. Paulo centenário (1594–1994) [Macau].
17.1995, 59–60
D. E. M.

161 Colloque in Würzburg: Martino Martini and the China Mission of the Jesuits in the 17th century. New results and perspectives in research.
17.1995, 60–61
Claudia von Collani, Würzburg

162 [rev.] Discovering China. European interpretations in the Enlightenment. Edited by Julia Ching and Willard Oxtoby. Rochester 1992. XXXI, 211 pp. (Library of the History of Ideas 7.) ISBN 1-878822-14-4
17.1995, 62–64
Claudia von Collani, Würzburg

163 [rev.] Ming history: An introductory guide to research. Compiled by Edward L. Farmer, Romeyn Taylor & Ann Waltner, with the assistance of Jiang Yonglin. Minneapolis 1994. VI, 451 pp. (Ming Studies Research Series 3.) ISBN 1-886108-02-1
17.1995, 65
D. E. M.

164 [rev.] The fascinating god. A challenge to modern Chinese theology presented by a text on the name of god written by a 17th century Chinese student of theology. By Nicolas Standaert SJ. Rome: Pontificia Università Gregoriana 1995. IX, 195 pp. (Inculturation. Working papers on living faith and cultures 17.)
17.1995, 66–68
D. E. M.

## 18.1996

165 The Zikawei 許家匯 Collection in the Jesuit Theologate Library at Fujen 輔仁 University (Taiwan); background and draft catalogue. By Adrian Dudink, Amsterdam.
18.1996, 1–40

166 [Philippe] Couplet's biography of Madame Candida Xu (1607–1680). By Gail King, Brigham Young University.
18.1996, 41–56

167 An addendum on Jesuit tombstones.
18.1996, 57–58
Susan Naquin, Princeton University

168 Publication of Chinese texts from Zikawei Library.
18.1996, 58

169 [rev.] [Chen Cunfu (ed.): Zongjiao yu wenhua luncong.][Religion and culture; collected essays.] 陳村富：宗教與文化論叢. Beijing: Dongfang chubanshe 1995. IV, 349 pp. ISBN 7-5060-0570-0
18.1996, 59–60
D. E. M.

170 [rev.] The liberating gospel in China. The Christian faith among China's minority peoples. By Ralph R. Covell. Grand Rapids, Michigan: Baker Books 1995. 318 pp., 5 maps. ISBN 0-8010-2595-8

18.1996, 60–61
D. E. M.

171 [rev.] The sanctuaries in a North China city. A complete survey of the cultic buildings in the
city of Hsüan-hua (Chahar). By the survey team of Fujen University (August 1948), Willem
A. Grootaers 賀登崧, Li Shih-yü 李世瑜 & Wang Fu-shih 王輔世. Brussels: Institut Belge
des Hautes Études Chinoises 1995. XIX, 245 pp. (Mélanges chinois et bouddhiques 26.) ISSN
0775-4612
18.1996, 61–62
D. E. M.

172 [rev.] Historiography of the Chinese Catholic church (nineteenth and twentieth centuries).
Edited by Jeroom Heyndrickx, C.I.C.M. Leuven: Ferdinand Verbiest Foundation 1994. 510
pp. (Louvain Chinese Studies 1.) ISBN 90-801833-2-6
18.1996, 62–63
D. E. M.

173 [rev.] Writings on China. By Gottfried Wilhelm Leibniz. Translated with an introduction,
notes and commentaries by Daniel J. Cook and Henry Rosemont, Jr. Chicago, La Salle, Ill.:
Open Court 1994. XX, 157 pp. ISBN 0-8126-9250-0
18.1996, 63–64
D. E. M.

174 [rev.] Sinica Franciscana. Volumen IX: Relationes et epistolae Fratrum Minorum Hispanorum
in Sinis qui annis 1697–98 missionem ingressi sunt. Compiled and annotated by Fr. Fortunato
Margiotti OFM; prepared for publication and corrected by the Frs. Gaspar Han & Antolin
Abad OFM. Rome: Segeretria delle Missioni 1995. CXX, 1127 pp. ISBN 84-7047-057-4
18.1996, 65–66
D. E. M.

175 [rev.] The Chinese Rites Controversy, its history and meaning. Edited by D. E. Mungello.
Nettetal: Steyler Verlag 1994. X, 356 pp. (Monumenta serica monograph series 33.) ISBN 3-
8050-0348-X
18.1996, 66–68
Lauren Pfister, Hong Kong Baptist University

176 [rev.] Inventaire sommaire des manuscrits et imprimés chinois de la Bibliothèque Vaticane.
By Paul Pelliot. Revised and edited by Takata Tokio. Foreword by Antonino Forte. Kyoto:
Istituto Italiano di Cultura, Scuola di studi sull' Asia Orientale 1995. XI, 113 pp. (Italian
School of East Asian Studies Reference Series 1.) ISBN 4-900793-10-8
18.1996, 68–70
D. E. M.

177 [rev.] Listy z Číny do vlasti a jiná korespondence s evropejskými hvězdáři (1716–1735)
[Letters from China to his native country and other correspondence with European
astronomers (1716–1735)]. By Karel Slavíček SJ. Edited and translated by Josef Kolmaš.
Prague. Vyšehrad 1994. 269 pp. ISBN 80-7021-127-X
18.1996, 70–71
D. E. M.

178 [rev.] God's Chinese son. The Taiping Heavenly Kingdom of Hong Xiuquan. By Jonathan
    Spence. New York: W. W. Norton 1996. XXVI, 400 pp. ISBN 0-393-03844-0
    18.1996, 71–73
    D. E. M.

179 [rev.] Ferdinand Verbiest (1623–1688). Jesuit missionary, scientist, engineer and diplomat.
    Edited by John W. Witek SJ. Nettetal: Steyler Verlag 1994. 602 pp. (Monumenta serica
    monograph series 30.) ISBN 3-8050-0328-5
    18.1996, 74–78
    John B. Henderson, Baton Rouge, Louisiana

180 [rev.] [Zhu Weizheng: Jidujiao yu jindai wenhua.][Christianity and modern culture.]
    朱維錚：基督教與近代文化. Shanghai: Shanghai Renmin chubanshe 1994. 489 pp. ISBN 7-
    208-01896-0
    18.1996, 79–80
    John Dragon Young, Lecturer in Legal Translation, Department of Translation, Chinese
    University of Hong Kong

## 19.1997

181 Necrology: Dr. John Dragon Young 楊意龍 (1949–1996).
    19.1997, 1–5

182 Andreas Ly on the first Jinchuan War in Western Sichuan (1747–1749). Translated by Robert
    Entenmann, St. Olaf College.
    19.1997, 6–21

183 Newly available Manchu documents pertaining to Sino-Western relations in the Kangxi
    period. By Eugenio Menegon, University of California, Berkeley.
    19.1997, 22–46
    [Listing according to *Kangxi chao Manwen shupi zouzhe quan yi*. Beijing 1996.]

184 [rev.] [Shengchao poxieji, by Xia Guiqi; ed. by Xu Changshi] 聲朝破邪集
    夏瑰琦編。徐昌治訂 .[A collection of writings attacking falsehood]. Hong Kong: Jiandao
    shenxueyuan 1996. 422 pp. ISBN 962-7997-06-4
    19.1997, 47–49
    D. E. M.

185 [rev.] [Xujiahui shulou Ming Qing tianzhujiao wenxian] 徐家匯書樓明清天主教文獻
    Chinese Christan texts from the Zikawei Library / Nicolas Standaert, Adrian Dudink, Huang
    Yinong. Taibei: Fuda shenxueyuan 1996. 5 vols. ISBN 957-98886-04
    19.1997, 49–55
    D. E. M.

186 [rev.] Departed, yet present. Zhalan, the oldest Christan cemetery in Beijing. Edited by
    Edward J. Malatesta SJ and Gao Zhiyu. Macao: Instituto Cultural de Macau and Ricci
    Institute of the University of San Francisco 1995. 315 pp., 135 ill. ISBN 972-35-0213-5
    19.1997, 55–59
    D. E. M.

187 [rev.] Jean-François Gerbillon SJ (1654–1707), un des cinq mathématiciens envoyés en Chine
    par Louis XIV. Par Mme Yves de Thomaz de Bossière. Leuven: Ferdinand Verbiest
    Foundation 1994. 211 pp. (Louvain Chinese Studies 2.) ISBN 90-801833-1-8
    19.1997, 59–63
    Rita Widmaier, Leibniz Archiv, Hannover

188 Symposium on the History of Christianity in China 中國基督教發展史學術研討會
    Hong Kong.
    19.1997, 64–66
    D. E. M.

189 Report on the research project "A Confucian Reflection on the Enlightenment Mentality".
    19.1997, 67–68
    Dominic Sachsenmaier, Cambridge & Freiburg


**20.1998**

190 Necrology: The Reverend Dr. Edward J. Malatesta SJ. (1932–1998).
    20.1998,1–9 [with bibliography]
    D. E. M.

191 Nekrolog: Prof. Dr. Bernward (Heinrich) Willeke OFM (1913–1997).
    20.1998, 9–12 [with selected bibliography]
    Claudia von Collani

192 E. C. Bridgman and the missionary roots of American Sinology. By Michael C. Lazich,
    Buffalo State College.
    20.1998, 13-33

193 Did Jesus Christ really come to China? By Claudia von Collani, Katholisch-theologische
    Fakultät, Universität Würzburg.
    20.1998, 34–48

194 Note on a late Ming dynasty Chinese description of "Ricci's Church" in Beijing. By Gail
    King, Brigham Young University, Provo, Utah.
    20.1998, 49–51

195 [rev.] Giuliano Bertuccioli e Federico Masini: Italia e China. Roma: Laterza 1996. VII, 366
    pp., 29 ill. ISBN 88-420-5088-1
    20.1998, 52–55
    Claudia von Collani

196 [rev.] W. South Coblin: Notes on the sound system of late Ming *guanhua*. *Monumenta serica*
    45.1997, 261–307.
    20.1998, 56
    D. E. M.

197 [rev.] Francesco d'Arelli: The Catholic mission in China in the 17th–18th centuries archives
    and libraries in Italy: preliminary repertoire. *East and West* 47.1997, 293–340.
    20.1998, 56–57
    D. E. M.

198 [rev.] [Fujian dui wai wenhua jiaoliu shi. Zhu bian Lin Jinshui.] 福建對外文化交流史。主編林金水. [The history of cultural relations between Fujian and foreign countries.] Fuzhou: Fujian jiaoyu chubanshe 1997. 487 pp. ISBN 7-5334-2030-6
20.1998, 57–58
D. E. M.

199 [rev.] China. Revised edition by Charles W. Hayford. Santa Barbara: ABC-CLIO 1997. 601 pp. ISBN 1-85109-235-8 (World bibliographical series 35.)
20.1998, 58–59
D. E. M.

200 [rev.] Matthias Klaue: Wider das Budeyi. Gelingen oder Scheitern einer christlich-konfuzanischen Synthese in der apologetischen Schrift *Budeyi Bian* (1665) des Jesuiten Ludovico Buglio. *Monumenta Serica* 45.1997, 101–259.
20.1998, 59
D. E. M.

201 [rev.] Western humanistic culture presented to China by Jesuit missionaries (XVII–XVIII centuries). Proceedings of the conference held in Rome, October 25–27, 1993. Edited by Federico Masini. Rome: Institutum Historicum SI. 1996. 396 pp. (Bibliotheca Instituti Historici SI. 49.) ISBN 88-7041-346-2
20.1998, 59–62
Robert Entenmann, St. Olaf College

202 [rev.] Matteo Ripa: Giornale (1705–1724).
Volume 1 (1705–1711). Introduzione, testo critico et note di Michele Fatica. Indici, glossario cinese. 29 tavole. Napoli: Istituto Universitario Orientale, Dipartimento di filosofia e Politica 1991. CLXX, 303 pp. (Istituto Universitario Orientale Collana Matteo Ripa 9.)
Volume 2 (1711–1716). Testo critico, note e appendice documentaria di Michele Fatica. 45 tavole. Indici. Napoli 1996. XX, 413 pp. (Collana Matteo Ripa 14.)
20.1998, 62–64
D. E. M.

203 [rev.] Sinica Franciscana. Volumen X: Relationes et epistolae Fratrum Minorum Hispanorum in Sinis qui annis 1696–98 missionem ingressi sunt. Compiled and annotated by Fr. Antonius S. Rosso OFM; prepared for publication and corrected by the Frs. Gaspar Han 韓承良 & Antolin Abad OFM. Madrid 1997. LXXVI, 1108 pp. ISBN 84-7047-062-0
20.1998, 64–65
D. E. M.

204 [rev.] Christianity in China. *The Catholic Historical Review* 83.1977, 569–690.
Wang Meixiu 王美秀: Niweisi di San zi zhu Zhang ji qi fanxiang 倪維思的 三自主張及其反響. *Shijie zongjiao yanjiu* 世界宗教研究 71.1998, 107–118.
20.1998, 65–66
D. E. M.

205 [rev.] Supplément à l'Inventaire des livres chinois de la Bibliothèque Vaticane. 梵蒂岡圖書館所藏漢籍目錄補編 [Fandigang tushuguan socang Hanji mulu bubian] par Takata Tokio 高田時雄編. Kyoto: Institute for Research in Humanities, Kyoto University 1997. VI, 68 pp. (Documentation Center for Oriental Studies, series 7.)

20.1998, 66
D. E. M.

206 [rev.] Pang Diwo yu Zhongguo: Yesuhui shiying celüe yanjiu. Zhang Kai zhu. Xibanya
Yesuhui Pang Diwo laihua 400 zhounian jinian. 龐迪我與中國 耶穌會 適應 策略研究
張鎧著 西班牙耶穌會龐迪我來華 400 週年記念 [400th anniversary of the Spanish Jesuit's
Diego de Pantoja arrival in China]. Beijing: Beijing tushuguan chubanshe 1997. 466,16 pp.
ISBN 7-5013-1427-6
Diego de Pantoja y China (1597–1618): un estudio sobre la Politica de Adaptación de la
Compañia de Jesús. / Zhang Kai. Commemoración del IV centenario de la llegada a China del
jesuita español Diego de Pantoja (1597–1997). Traducción al español: Tang Baisheng y Kang
Xiaolin. Beijing: Editorial de la biblioteca de Beijing 1997. 180 pp. ISBN 7-5013-1443-8
20.1998, 67–68
D. E. M.

207 International Colloquium: Matteo Ripa. The Catholic mission in China (18th century) and the
«Collegio de Cinesi» of Naples. Istituto Universitario Orientale, Napoli, February 11–12,
1997.
20.1998, 69–71
D. E. M.

208 International Symposium: 300 Jahre Novis*sima Sinica*. Technische Universität Berlin, 4.–7.
Oktober 1997.
20.1998, 71–73
D. E. M.

209 Europe in China III. Berlin, 22–26 April 1998.
20.1998, 73–76
Nicolas Standaert, Katholieke Universiteit Leuven


**21.1999**

210 Necrology – le Père Yves Raguin 甘易逢神父 (1912–1998).
21.1999, 1–4
Original French text composed by Yves Camus SJ. Translated by D. E. M.
3–4: A selected bibliography of published works.

211 The Archives des Missions Étrangères de Paris – AMEP and their Chinese holdings. By
Eugenio Menegon, University of California, Berkeley.
21.1999, 5–8

212 A Chinese translation of Ambroise Paré's Anatomy. By Nicolas Standaert, K. U. Leuven.
21.1999, 9–33

New publications in the field
213 Review article *Monumenta serica monograph series*.
"Western learning" and Christianity in China: The contribution and impact of Johann Adam
Schall von Bell (1592–1666). Edited by Roman Malek SVD. Nettetal: Steyler Verlag 1998. 2
vols., 1259 pp. 165 ills. (Monumenta serica monograph series 35.)
Il natural lume de Cinese. Teoria e prasi dell'evangelizzazione in Cina nelle breve relatione di

Philippe Couplet S.J. (1623–1693). By Secondino Gatta. Edited by Roman Malek with assistance from Katharina Feith. Nettetal: Steyler Verlag 1998. 241 pp., facsimile of original Italian text from Archivum Romanum Societatis Iesu, Jap. Sin. 131. (Monumenta serica monograph series 27.)

"Scholar from the West": Giulio Aleni SJ. (1582–1649) and the dialogue between Christianity and China. Edited by Tiziana Lippiello and Roman Malek. Nettetal: Steyler Verlag 1997. XXVI, 671 pp., 14 Ill., 3 maps, 3 tables & index with Chinese character glossary. (Monumenta serica monograph series 42; Fondazione Civiltà Bresciana, Annali 9.)

Bible in modern China: The literary and intellectual impact. Edited by Irene Eber, Sze-kar Wan & Knut Walf in collaboration with Roman Malek. Nettetal: Steyler Verlag 1999. 450 pp. (Monumenta serica monograph series 43.)

Jews and Judaism in traditional China. A comprehensive bibliography. By Donald Daniel Leslie. Nettetal: Steyler Verlag 1998. 291 pp., 13 ills., index with Chinese character glossary. (Monumenta serica monograph series 44.)

21.1999, 34–43

D. E. M.


214 [rev.] The Chan's great continent: China in western minds by Jonathan D. Spence. New York: W. W. Norton 1998. XVIII,279 pp.

21.1999, 43–47

D. E. M.


215 [rev.] ["Zhongguo liyi zhi zheng; lishi, wenxian he yiyi" Li Tiangang zhu] "中國禮儀之爭。歷史, 文獻和意義" 李天綱著. [The Chinese Rites Controversy: history, documents and meaning.] 上海：上海古籍出版社 1998. 389 pp.

21.1999, 47–48

D. E. M.


216 [rev.] Christianity in China, from the eighteenth century to the present. Edited by Daniel H. Bays. Stanford: Stanford University Press 1996. XXII, 483 pp.

21.1999, 48–49

D. E. M.


217 [rev.] The Golden Needle. The biography of Frederick Stewart (1836–1889) by Gillian Bickley. Hong Kong: David C. Lam Institute for East-West Studies, Hong Kong Baptist University 1997. XI, 307 pp.

21.1999, 49–50

D. E. M.


218 [rev.] Macau and Sino-Portuguese relations, ca. 1513/14 to ca. 1900: A bibliographical essay, by Roderich Ptak. *Monumenta Serica* 46 (1998), 343–396.

21.1999, 50–51

Gail King, University of Brigham Young


219 The Ming-Qing conflict, 1619–1683. A historiography and source guide by Lynn A. Struve. Ann Arbor: Association for Asian Studies 1998. (AAS monograph and occasional paper series 56.)

21.1999, 51–53

Gail King, University of Brigham Young

220 Manufacturing Confucianism: Chinese traditions and universal civilization by Lionel M.
    Jensen. Durham, London: Duke University Press 1997. XIX,444 pp., 13 ills.
    21.1999, 53–57
    On-cho Ng, The Pennsylvania State University

221 Opera Omnia. By Martino Martini S.J. Edited by Giuliano Bertuccioli. Editorial direction by
    Franco Demarchi. Trento: Università di Trento 1998.
    Volume I: Lettere e documenti. 547 pp., 20 ills., 9 maps. chronology of the life and works of
    Martini, list of Chinese characters.
    Volume II: Opere minori. 516 pp., 17 ills., lists of Chinese characters.
    21.1999, 57–58
    D. E. M.

222 Notable doctoral dissertation:
    Die Aufnahme europäischer Inhalte in die chinesische Kultur durch Zhu Zongyuan (ca. 1616–
    1660) vorgelegt von Dominic Sachsenmaier.  Freiburg i. Br. 1998/99. 253 pp.
    21.1999, 59–60
    D. E. M.

223 International Conference on Wang Tao and the Modern World.
    21.1999, 60


**22.2000**


224 張星曜 "欽命傳教約述" (Zhang Xingyao and the Collected Discussions on the Imperial
    Decrees concerning the Missionaries) / 韓琦 (Han Qi).
    22.2000, 1–10

225 Notizen aus dem Leibniz-Archiv Hannover / Rita Widmaier, Hannover.
    22.2000, 10–12
    1. Leibniz' Fragment der Elementa linguae tartaricae von Ferdinand Verbiest SJ.
    2. Niccolò Longobardis Traité sur quelques points de la religion de Chinois.

226 Christian charity in seventeenth-century China / Gail King, Brigham Young University.
    22.2000, 13–30

227 The Biblioteca Casatanense (Rome) and its China materials. A finding list, by Eugenio
    Menegon, University of California, Berkeley.
    22.2000, 31–55

228 Review article: Inculturation versus evangelization: Are contemporary values causing us to
    misinterpret the 16–18th century Jesuit missionaries?
    Art on the Jesuit missions in Asia and Latin America, 1542–1773. By Gauvin Alexander
    Bailey. Toronto, Buffalo, London: University of Toronto Press 1999. XII, 310 pp. ISBN 0-
    8020-4688-6
    22.2000, 56–60
    Jonathan Chaves, The George Washington University

New publications in the field

229 [rev.] Preaching Christ in late Ming China: The Jesuit presentation of Christ from Matteo Ricci to Giulio Aleni by Gianni Criveller. Originally presented as a disstertion to Pontificia Facoltà Teologica dell'Italia Meridionale. Taipei, Brescia: Taipei Ricci Institute, in collaboration with Fondazione Civiltà Bresciana 1997. XXIV,479 pp. (Variétés sinologiques NS 86; Fondazione Civiltà Bresciana, Annali 10.)
22.2000, 61–63
D. E. M.

230 [rev.] Matteo Ripa e il Collegio dei Cinesi. La Missione cattolica in Cina tra secoli XVIII–XIX. Atti del Colloquio Internationale, Napoli, 11–12 febbraio 1997, a cura die Michele Fatica e Francesco d'Arelli. Napoli 1999. X,488 pp. (Istituto Universitario Orientale di Napoli. Collana "Matteo Ripa" 16.)
22.2000, 63–64
D. E. M.

231 [rev.] The Christian mission in China in the Verbiest era: Some aspects of the missionary approach edited by Noel Golvers. Leuven: Leuven University Press, Ferdinand Verbiest Foundation 1999. 114 pp. (Louvain Chinese studies 6.)
22.2000, 64–65
D. E. M.

232 [rev.] François de Rougemont, SJ, missionary in Ch'ang-shu (Chiang-nan). A study of the account book (1674–1676) and the elogium by Noel Golvers. Leuven: Leuven University Press, Ferdinand Verbiest Foundation 1999. XVII, 794 pp. (Louvain Chinese studies 7.)
22.2000, 65–67
D. E. M.

233 [rev.] [Laibunici he ruxue. Meng Dewei [Mungello] zhu, Zhang Xuezhi yi] 萊布尼慈和儒學. [Leibniz and Confucianism.] （美）孟德衛著。張學智譯。 南京：江蘇人民出版社 1998. 2,139 pp. （海外中國研究叢書）
22.2000, 67
D. E. M.

234 [rev.] The Bible in China. The history of the Union Version or the culminant of Protestant missionary bible translation in China by Jost Oliver Zetzsche. Nettetal: Steyler Verlag 1999. 456 pp., 13 ills. (Monumenta serica monograph series 45.)
22.2000, 67–69
D. E. M.

235 [rev.] Joanna Waley-Cohen: The sextants of Beijing. Global currents in Chinese history. New York: W. W. Norton 1999. IX, 322 pp., 4 maps.
22.2000, 70–79
Lionel M. Jensen, University of Notre Dame

236 [rev.] Andrius Rudomina – XVII a. Lietuvos religinės kulturos atstovas by Eglė Sadzevičiutė. *Lietuviu Kataliku Mokslo Akademija. Metraštis* 13 (1998), 239–339.
22.2000, 79–80
Hartmut Walravens, Berlin

**23.2001**

237 Necrology: Professor Dr. Donald F. Lach 勞端納教授 (1917–2000).
23.2001, 1–7
Theodore Nicholas Foss, The University of Chicago

238 Fact and fantasy in the sexual seduction of Chinese converts by Catholic priests: the case of
the 120 martyrs. / D. E. Mungello 孟德衛 Baylor University.
23.2001, 8–21

239 A missionary philosopher of the late Qing: Ernst Faber and his intercultural synthesis of
human nature. / Gad C. Isay, The Hebrew University of Jerusalem.
23.2001, 22–49

240 European astrology in early Qing China: Xue Fengzuo's and Smogulecki's translation of
Cardano's commentaries on Ptolemy's *Tetrabiblos* / Nicolas Standaert 鐘鳴旦 Katholieke
Universiteit Leuven.
23.2001, 50–79

New publications in the field
241 [rev.] Das Neueste über China: G. W. Leibnizens *Novissima Sinica* von 1697. Wenchao Li
and Hans Poser, Hrsg. Stuttgart: Franz Steiner 2000. 390 pp. (Studia Leibnitiana Supplementa
33.)
23.2001, 80–86.
Haun Saussy, Stanford University

242 [rev.] Michael C. Lazich: E. C. Bridgman (1801–1861), America's first missionary to China.
Lewiston: Edwin Mellen 2000. V, 400 pp. (Studies in the history of missions 19.)
23.2001, 86–88
Kathleen L. Lodwick, Pennsylvania State University

243 [rev.] Handbook of Christianity in China. Volume One: 635–1800. Edited by Nicolas
Standaert. Leiden: Brill 2001. XXVII,964 pp. (Handbuch der Orientalistik. Section 4: China,
vol. 15,1.)
23.2001, 89–90
D. E. M.

244 [rev.] *Chinesia*: The European construction of China in the literature of the 17th and 18th
centuries. By Adrian Hsia. Tübingen: Max Niemeyer 1998. IV, 144 pp. (Communicatio 16.)
The vision of China in the English literature of the seventeenth and eighteenth centuries.
Edited by Adrian Hsia. Hong Kong: The Chinese University Press 1998. XI, 404 pp.
23.2001, 90–92
D. E. M.

245 [rev.] China and Christianity. Burdened past, hopeful future. Edited by Stephan Uhalley, Jr. &
Xiaoxin Wu. Armonk, New York: M. E. Sharpe 2000. XIII, 499 pp.
23.2001, 92
D. E. M.

**24.2002**

246 Necrology: Professor Giuliano Bertuccioli 伯佐良教授 (1923–2001).
24.2002, 1–3
Federico Masini, with the cooperation of Marina Miranda and Bruno Bertuccioli, edited by D.
E. Mungello

247 Preliminary bibliography [of Bertuccioli], compiled by D. E. Mungello.
24.2002, 4–5

248 Gathering tea for god / Jonathan Chaves 齊皎翰, The George Washington University.
24.2002, 6–23
[Shengjiao caicha ge 聖教採茶歌, Catholic tea-gatherers' songs]

249 Portrait of an emperor: Joachim Bouvet's picture of the Kangxi emperor of 1697 / Claudia
von Collani 柯蘭易 Universität Würzburg.
24.2002, 24–37

250 *Tianzhu jiaoyao* 天主教要, the catechism (1605) published by Matteo Ricci. By Adrian
Dudink 杜鼎克 Catholic University of Leuven, Belgium.
24.2002, 38–50

New publications in the field
251 [rev.] Albert Chan SJ: Chinese books and documents in the Jesuit Archives in Rome. A
descriptive catalogue. Japonica-Sinica I–IV. Armonk, N.Y.: M. E. Sharpe 2002. XLIII, 627
pp.
24.2002, 51–52
D. E. M.

252 [rev.] Ryan Dunch: Fuzhou Protestants and the making of modern China, 1857–1927. New
Haven: Yale University Press 2001. XXI, 293 pp., 3 maps, 3 tables, 33 ills.
24.2002, 53–56
D. E. M.

253 [rev.] Bernhard Führer: Vergessen und verloren. Die Geschichte der österreichischen
Chinastudien. Bochum: Projekt-Verlag 2001. VI, 372 pp. (Edition Cathay 42.)
24.2002, 57–58

254 [rev.] Patrick Hanan: The missionary novels of nineteenth-century China. *Harvard Journal of
Asiatic Studies* 60 (2000), 413–443.
24.2002, 58
D. E. M.

255 [rev.] Laura Hostetler: Qing colonial enterprise. Ethnography and cartography in early
modern China. Chicago: University of Chicago Press 2001. XX, 258 pp.
24.2002, 59–61
D. E. M.

256 [rev.] Wenchao Li: Die christliche China-Mission im 17. Jahrhundert: Verständnis,
Unverständnis, Mißverständnis. Eine geistesgeschichtliche Studie zum Christentum,

Buddhismus und Konfuzianismus. Stuttgart: Franz Steiner 2000. 648 pp. (Studia Leibnitiana Supplementa 32.)

李文潮 [Li Wenchao] 波塞爾 [Hans Poser] 編。萊布尼茨與中國 — 中國近世 發表300週年國際學術討論會論文集（簡體）. [Laibunici yu Zhongguo – Zhongguo jinshi fabiao 300 zhounian kuoji xueshu taolun huilun wenji. Leibniz's Novissima Sinica of 1697. Proceedings of an international symposium.] 中國科學中心 (Chinesisch-Deutsches Zentrum für Wissenschaftsförderung). 北京：科學出版社 2002. VIII,365 pp. ISBN 7030098846

24.2002, 61–62
D. E. M.


257 [rev.] Catherine Jami, Peter Engelfriet and Gregory Blue, eds.: Statecraft and intellectual renewal in late Ming China. The cultural synthesis of Xu Guangqi (1562–1633). Leiden: Brill 2001. X,466 pp. (Sinica Leidensia 50.)
24.2002, 63–64
D. E. M.


258 [rev.] Ku Wei-ying 古偉瀛, ed.: Missionary approaches and linguistics in mainland China and Taiwan. Leuven: Leuven University Press 2001. 275 pp. (Leuven Chinese studies 10.)
24.2002, 64–65
D. E. M.


259 [rev.] Colin MacKerras, ed.: Sinophiles and Sinophobes. Western views of China. Oxford, New York: Oxford University Press 2000. XXVI,268 pp.
24.2002, 65–67
D. E. M.


260 [rev.] Roman Malek, Arnold Zingerle, eds.: Martino Martini S.J. (1614–1661) und die Chinamission im 17. Jahrhundert. Nettetal: Steyler Verlag 2000. 260 pp., 5 maps, 27 ills., 2 tables.
24.2002, 68
D. E. M.


261 [rev.] Roman Malek, ed.: Macau. Herkunft ist Zukunft. Nettetal: Steyler Verlag 2000. XVIII, 666 pp.
24.2002, 68–69
D. E. M.


262 [rev.] Roman Malek, ed.: From Kaifeng … to Shanghai. Jews in China. Nettetal: Steyler Verlag 2000. 706 pp. (Monumenta serica monograph series 46.)
24.2002, 69
D. E. M.


263 [rev.] Dominic Sachsenmaier: Die Aufnahme europäischer Inhalte in die chinesische Kultur durch Zhu Zhongyuan (ca. 1616–1666). Nettetal: Steyler Verlag 2001. 472 pp. (Monumenta serica monograph series 47.)
24.2002, 70–72
D. E. M.


264 [rev.][Shen Dingping: Ming Qing zhi ji zhongxi wenhua jiaoliu shi. Mingdai diaoshi yu shehui][The history of the Sino-Western cultural relations in the Ming Qing period.]

沈定評著. 明清之際中西文化交流史。明代調適與社會. 北京：商務印書館 2001. 750 pp.
ISBN 978-7-100-08703-2
24.2002, 72
D. E. M.

265 [rev.] Alan Richard Sweeten: Christianity in rural China: Conflict and accommodation in
Jiangxi Province, 1860–1900. Ann Arbor: Center for Chinese Studies, University of Michigan
2001. XII, 281 pp. (Michigan monographs in Chinese studies 91.) ISBN 0-89264-146-0
24.2002, 73–75
Ryan Dunch, University of Alberta

266 [rev.] Letter to the editor [Sept. 13, 2001]. [on comments in the review of his books.]
24.2002, 76
Adrian Hsia, McGill University


**25.2003**

267 On the 25th anniversary of the Sino-Western Cultural Relations Journal.
25.2003, 1–2
D. E. M.

268 [Letter to the editor [Dec. 6, 2002].
25.2003, 3
Wm. Theodore de Bary, Columbia University

269 [Letter by Han Qi, April 28, 2003].
25.2003, 4–5

270 [Letter to the editor, April 28, 2003].
25.2003, 5
J. S. Cummins, London University

271 Thoughts on the Sino-Western Cultural Relations Journal.
25.2003, 6–8
Jonathan Chaves, George Washington University

272 Necrology: Edwin J. Van Kley 范克雷 (1930–2002).
25.2003, 9–15
Theodore Nicholas Foss, University of Chicago

273 Xujiahui 徐家匯 (Zikawei) Library in Shanghai reopened.
25.2003, 15

274 Der Neue Welt-Bott. A preliminary survey. By Claudia von Collani, Universität Würzburg.
25.2003, 16–43

New publications in the field
275 [rev.] Michel Cartier: La Chine entre amour et haine. Paris: Desclée de Brouwer 1998. 452 pp.
(Actes du VIIIe Colloque de sinologie de Chantilly. Variétés sinologiques 87.)

25.2003, 44–45
D. E. M.

276 [rev.] Joseph Dehergne SJ et al.: Catéchisme et catecheses des Jésuites de Chine de 1584 à
     1800. *Monumenta Serica* 47 (1999), 397–478.
     25.2003, 45–46
     D. E. M.

277 [rev.] Antonino Forte and Federico Masini, eds.: A life journey to the East. Sinological
     studies in memory of Giuliano Bertuccioli (1923–2001). Italian School of East Asian Studies.
     Essays: Volume 2. Kyoto: Scuola Italiana sull'Asia Orientale 2002. XXXV, 280 pp. ISBN 4-
     900793-20-5
     25.2003, 46–47
     D. E. M.

278 [rev.] Noel Golvers: Ferdinand Verbiest SJ. (1623–1688) and the Chinese heaven. The
     composition of the astronomical corpus, its diffusion and reception in the European Republic
     of Letters. Leuven University Press & Ferdinand Verbiest Foundation 2002. 670 pp., ca. 60
     Illustrationen, 6 tab., 4 maps. (Leuven Chinese Studies 12.) ISBN 90-5867-293-X
     25.2003, 47–48
     D. E. M.

279 [rev.] Gottfried von Laimbeckhoven SJ (1707–1787), der Bischof von Nanjing und seine
     Briefe aus China mit Faksimile seiner Reisebeschreibung. Transkribiert und bearbeitet von
     Stephan Puhl (1941–1997) und Sigismund Freiherr Elverfeldt-Ulm unter Mitwirkung von
     Gerhard Zeilinger. Zum Druck vorbereitet und herausgegeben von Roman Malek SVD.
     Institut Monumenta Serica, St. Augustin. Nettetal: Steyler Verlag 2000. 492 pp. ISBN 3-
     8050-0442-7
     25.2003, 48

280 [rev.] Gottfried Wilhelm Leibniz: Discours sur la theologie naturelle des Chinois. Traité sur
     quelques points importans de la Mission de Chine von Antoine de Sainte Marie; Entretien
     d'un philosophe chrétien et d'un philosophe chinois sur l'existence et la nature de dieu von
     Nicolas Malebranche; Marginalien zu den Texten von Longobardi, Sainte Marie und
     Malebranche von Leibniz; Rezensionen aus dem Journal des Sçavans & Annotationes de
     cultu religioneque Sinensium von Leibniz. Herausgegeben und mit Anmerkungen versehen
     von Wenchao Li und Hans Poser. Frankfurt am Main: Vittorio Klostermann 2002. 308 pp., 32
     pl. (Veröffentlichungen des Leibniz-Archivs 13.) ISBN 3-465-03214-4
     25.2003, 48–49
     D. E. M.

281 [rev.] Cécile Leung: Etienne Fourmont (1683–1745). Oriental and Chinese languages in
     eighteenth-century France. Leuven University Press & Verbiest Foundation 2002. 314 pp., 8
     ill., 2 tab., 5 append. (Leuven Chinese Studies 13.) ISBN 90-5867-248-4
     25.2003, 49–53
     Jocelyn M. N. Marinescu, Kansas State University

282 [rev.] Lin Xiaoping: Wu Li (1632–1718). His life, his paintings. Lanham, Maryland 2001.
     XVII, 217 pp. ISBN 0-7618-1843-X
     25.2003, 53–55
     D. E. M.

283 [rev.] Martino Martini S.J.: Opera Omnia; edizione diretta da Franco Demarchi. Volume 3:
Novus Atlas Sinensis, a cura di Giuliano Bertuccioli. Trento: Università di Trento 2002. 2
Bücher. 1175 pp. ISBN 88-8443-028-3
25.2003, 55
D. E. M.

284 [rev.] Roman Malek SVD, ed.: The Chinese face of Jesus Christ. Vol. 1. Jointly published by
Institut Monumenta Serica and China-Zentrum, St. Augustin. Nettetal: Steyler Verlag 2002.
391 pp. (Monumenta Serica Monograph series 50,1.) ISBN 3-8050-0477-X
25.2003, 55–56
D. E. M.

285 [rev.] Eugenio Menegon: Ancestors, virgins and friars. The localization of Christianity in late
imperial Mindong (Fujian, China) 1632–1863. Doctoral dissertation in History at the
University of California, Berkeley. Committee chair: Professor Frederic E. Wakeman Jr.
Spring 2002. 379 pp.
Catherine Pagani: Eastern magnificence & European ingenuity: Clocks of late imperial China.
Ann Arbor: The University of Michigan Press 2001. XVI, 286 pp. ISBN 0-472-11208-2
25.2003, 56–60
Laura Hostetler, University of Illinois, Chicago

286 [rev.] David Porter: Ideographia. The Chinese cipher in early modern Europe. Stanford,
California: Stanford University Press 2001. 312 pp. ISBN 0-8048-3203-5
25.2003, 60–64
John W. Witek SJ

287 [rev.] Matteo Ricci: Lettere (1580–1609), edited by Francesco d'Arelli. Macerata: Quodlibet
2001. LV, 617 pp. ISBN 88-86570-65-1
25.2003, 64–69
Eugenio Menegon, Katholieke Universiteit Leuven

288 [rev.] Luís Saraiva, ed.: History of mathematical sciences: Portugal and East Asia II.
Scientific papers and the Portuguese expansion in Asia (1498–1759). Papers from the
international meeting organized by the University of Macao and the Centro de Matemática e
Aplicações Fundamentais, Universidade de Lisboa, Macau, 10–12 October 1998. Lisbon
2011. XIV, 182 pp. ISBN 972-95229-3-6
25.2003, 69–70
D. E. M.

289 [rev.] Nicolas Standaert, Adrian Dudink 杜鼎克, eds.: Chinese Christian texts from the
Roman Archives of the Society of Jesus. Taipei: Ricci Institute Taipei 2002. 12 vols. ISBN
957-9390-16-9
25.2003, 70–71
D. E. M.

290 [rev.] John W. Witek SJ and †Joseph S. Sebes SJ, eds.: Monumenta Sinica. 1 (1546–1562).
Rome: Institutum Historicum Societatis Iesu 2002. 498 pp. (Monumenta Historica Societatis
Iesu 153.) ISBN 88-7041-153-6
25.2003, 71–72
D. E. M.

## 26.2004

291 Julia Ching 秦家懿 [Qin Jiayi] (1934–2001).
    26.2004, 1–7
    D. E. M.

292 Publications [of Julia Ching].
    26.2004, 8–12

293 Chinese flora presented to seventeenth-century Europe: a "taste of foreign fruit from the
    Chinese garden". By Bianca Maria Rinaldi, University of Hannover.
    26.2004, 13–45

294 The Chinese Christian books of the former Beitang Library. By Adrian Dudink 杜鼎克,
    Katholieke Universiteit Leuven.
    26.2004, 46–59

295 For the instruction of those aspiring to be Christians: João Soerio's *Tianzhu shengjiao yueyan*
    天主聖教約言. By Gail King, Brigham Young University.
    26.2004, 59–67

296 [rev.] Norman J. Girardot: The Victorian translation of China: James Legge's Oriental
    Pilgrimage. Berkeley: University of California Press 2002. XXX,780 pp., 38 ill. ISBN 0-520-
    21552-4
    26.2004, 68–72
    R. G. Tiedemann 狄德滿, University of London

297 [rev.] [Qing zhongqianqi xiyang tianzhujiao zai hua huodong dang'an shiliao] 清
    中前期西洋天主教在華活動檔案史料 (Archives concerning Western Catholic Missions
    from the early to mid Qing Dynasty in China). Ed.: China No. 1 Historical Archive. Beijing:
    Zhonghua shuju 2003. 4 vols. ISBN 7-101-03958-8
    26.2004,72–73
    Gail King 歐凱泥, Brigham Young University

298 [rev.] Roman Malek SVD, ed.: The Chinese face of Jesus Christ. Vol. 2, jointly published by
    Institut Monumenta Serica and China-Zentrum, St. Augustin. Nettetal: Steyler Verlag 2003.
    pp. 393–844. (Monumenta serica monograph series 50,2.) ISBN 3-8050-0478-8
    26.2004, 73
    D. E. M.

299 [rev.]. Karl Josef Rivinius: Das Collegium Sinicum zu Neapel und seine Umwandlung in ein
    Orientalisches Institut. Ein Beitrag zu seiner Geschichte. Nettetal: Steyler Verlag 2004. 174
    pp. (Collectanea Serica.) ISBN 3-8050-0498-2
    26.2004, 73–74
    D. E. M.

300 [rev.] Christian Stücken: Der Mandarin des Himmels. Zeit und Leben des Chinamissionars
    Ignaz Kögler SJ (1680–1746). Nettetal: Steyler Verlag 2003. 440 pp., 23 Ill. (Collectanea
    Serica.) ISBN 3-8050-0488-5

26.2004,74–76
D. E. M.

301 [rev.] Patrick Taveirne: Han-Mongol encounters and missionary endeavor. A history of Scheut in Ordos (Hetao) 1874–1911. Leuven: Leuven University Press 2004. 684 pp., 6 Kt., 10 farb. Ill. (Leuven Chinese Studies 15.) ISBN 90-5867-365-0
26.2004, 76
D. E. M.

302 [rev.] W. F. Vande Walle & Noël Golvers, ed.: The history of the relations between the Low Countries and China in the Qing era (1644–1911). Leuven: Leuven University Press 2003. 508 pp. (Leuven Chinese Studies 14.) ISBN 90-5867-315-4
26.2004, 76
D. E. M.

**27. 2005**

303 Necrology: Albert Chan, S.J. 陳綸緒神父 (1915–2005).
27.2005, 1–8
D. E. M.
With Preliminary bibliography, compiled by Mark Mir & D. E. M.

304 The return of the Jesuits to China in 1841 and the Chinese Christian backlash. By D. E. Mungello 孟德衞.
27.2005, 9–46

305 [rev.] Elisabetta Corsi: La fábrica de las illusiones. Los Jesuitas y la difusión de la perspectiva lineal en China, 1698–1766. México: El Colegio de México, Centro de Estudios de Asia y África 2004. 242 pp., 15 color pl. ISBN 968-12-1125-1
27.2005, 47–50
D. E. M.

306 [rev.] Thoralf Klein and Reinhard Zöllner, eds.: Karl Gützlaff (1803–1851) und das Christentum in Ostasien. Ein Missionar zwischen den Kulturen. A collection of ten papers presented at a conference in commemoration of Gützlaff's 150th Todesjahr held at the Universität Erfurt in 2001. Nettetal: Steyler Verlag 2005. 376 pp. (Collectanea Serica.) ISBN 3-8050-0520-2
27.2005, 50–53
D. E. M.

307 [rev.] Franklin Perkins: Leibniz and China. A commerce of light. Cambridge: Cambridge University Press 2004. XVIII, 224 pp., 1 map.
27.2005, 53–56
Daniel J. Cook, Brooklyn College, CUNY

308 [rev.] Zbigniew Wesołowski SVD 魏思齊, ed.: Monumenta Serica. Journal of Oriental Studies 華裔學志。中譯標題目錄 1–50 冊 (1935–2002). A catalogue of titles and contents, volumes 1–50 (1935–2002) with Chinese translation. 輔仁大學出版社 2004. 423 pp.

27.2005, 56
D. E. M.

## 28.2006

309 Lubelli's *Wanmin simo tu* 萬民四末圖 (Picture of the Four Last Things of All People), ca.
    1683. By Adrian Dudink 杜鼎克, Catholic University of Leuven.
    28.2006, 1–17

310 Necrology: Professor Dr. Arnulf Pierre Camps, OFM 甘柏主教授 (1925–2006).
    28.2006, 18

311 The *Ruijianlu* 睿鑒錄 (Record of Sage Scrutiny) and its role in the defense of Christianity in
    the early Qianlong era. By Jocelyn M. N. Marinescu 倪卓熙, Kansas State University.
    28.2006, 19–36

312 Index der Biographien in Fang Haos *Zhongguo Tianzhujiao shi renwu zhuan*
    中國天主教史人物傳 [Biographies from the history of the Catholic Church in China, 1967–
    1973] by Roman Malek 馬雷凱.
    28.2006, 37–64

313 Archives of the diocese of Northern Shanxi (Taiyuan) 山西北教區檔案 [Shanxi beijiaoqu
    dang'an] 1900–1949 in the collection of Father Li Jianhua 李建華, Taiyuan Cathedral,
    Taiyuan, Shanxi. By Henrietta Harrison 沈艾娣, Harvard University.
    28.2006, 65–69

314 [rev.] Jean François Billeter: Contre François Jullien. Paris: Editions Allia 2006. 123 pp.
    ISBN 2-84485-216-5
    Isabelle Landry-Deron: La prevue par la Chine. La Description de J.-B. Du Halde, jésuite,
    1735. Paris: Éditions de l'École des hautes études en sciences sociales 2002. 428 pp. ISBN 2-
    7132-1426-2
    28.2006, 70–73
    D. E. M.

315 [rev.] Huang Yinong 黃一農: Liangtoushe – Mingmo Qingchu di diyidai tianzhujiao tu [The
    Two-Headed Snake – the first generation of Christians at the end of the Ming, beginning of
    the Qing period.] 兩頭蛇：明末清初旳第一代天主教徒。新竹市：清大出版社 2005.
    567 pp. ISBN 957-29880-8-5
    28.2006, 74–76
    D. E. M.

316 [rev.] Ezra Pound and Confucianism: Remaking humanism in the face of modernity by Feng
    Lan. Toronto: University of Toronto Press 2005. VII, 245 pp. ISBN 0-8020-8941-0
    28.2006, 76–80
    Jocelyn M. N. Marinescu, Kansas State University

317 [rev.] Joachim Bouvet SJ: Journal des voyages. Edited by Claudia von Collani. Taipei: Ricci
    Institute 2005. 8, 374 pp. (Variétés sinologiques NS 95.) ISBN 957-9390-79-7

28.2006, 81
D. E. M.

318 [rev.] Xiaoxin Wu, ed.: Encounters and dialogues. Changing perspectives on Chinese-Western exchanges from the sixteenth to the eighteenth centuries. Jointly published by Monumenta Serica Institute, Sankt Augustin, and the Ricci Institute of Chinese-Western Cultural History at the University of San Francisco. Nettetal: Steyler Verlag 2005. 402 pp. ISBN 3-8050-0525-8
28.2006, 82
D. E. M.

319 [rev.] W. South Coblin: Francisco Varo's Glossary of the Mandarin language. Vol. 1: An English and Chinese annotation of the Vovabulario de la lengua Mandarina. Vol. 2: Pinyin and English index of the vocabulario de la lengua Mandarina. Nettetal: Steyler Verlag 2006. 1003 pp. (Monumenta Serica Monograph Series 53.) ISBN 3-8050-0526-1
28.2006, 83
D. E. M.

320 [rev.] Giuseppe Tucci: Italia e Oriente. Edited by Francesco d'Arelli. Rome: Istituto Italiano per l'Africa e l'Oriente 2005. 211 pp. ISBN 88-85320-35-X
28.2006, 84
D. E. M.


## 29.2007

321 An eighteenth-century poem on infanticide by Chiang Shih-ch'üan (Jiang Shiquan) 蔣士銓. By Jonathan Chaves 齊皎翰, The George Washington University.
29.2007, 1–13

322 Chang Jui-t'u (Zhang Ruitu) 張瑞圖 (1570–1641) Poem in honor of Giulio Aleni SJ (1582–1649). By Jonathan Chaves 齊皎瀚, The George Washington University.
29.2007, 14–18

323 The sad tale of Lucio Wu 吳露爵 (1713–1763). By D. E. Mungello 孟德衛, Baylor University.
29.2007, 19–33

324 Note on the restored site (2003) of Xu Guangqi's tomb at Shanghai. By Adrian Dudink 杜鼎克, Catholic University of Leuven.
29.2007, 34–37

325 A journey to the East that never leaves Rome.
[rev.] Liam Matthew Brockey: Journey to the East: the Jesuit Mission to China, 1579–1724. Cambridge, Mass.: Harvard University 2007. XII, 496 pp. ISBN 0-674-02338-6
[rev.] Han Qi 韓琦, Wu Min 吳旻, ed.: Xichao chongzheng ji: Xichao ding'an: wai sanzhong [The veneration of our glorious [Ming] dynasty. Judgments of our glorious [Qing] dynasty] 熙朝崇正集： 熙朝定案： 外三種. Beijing: Zhonghua shuju 2006. 437 pp. (Zhongwai jiaotong shiji congkan.) ISBN 7-101-05142-1

29.2007, 38–44
D. E. M.

326 [rev.] John M. Carroll: A concise history of Hong Kong. Lanham, Md.: Rowman and
     Littlefield 2007. XI, 270 pp. ISBN 0-7425-3421-9
     29.2007, 45–46
     D. E. M.

327 [rev.] Ad Dudink: Chinese books and documents (pre-1900) in the Royal Library of Belgium
     at Brussels. Brussels: Archives et Bibliothèques de Belgique 2006. 166 pp. (Inventaires 12.)
     ISSN 0775-0722
     29.2007, 46–47
     D. E. M.

328 [rev.] Huang Xiaojuan 黃曉鵑: Christian communities and alternative devotions in China,
     1780–1860. Doctoral dissertation in East Asian Studies at Princeton University. Academic
     advisor: Professor Susan Naquin. 2006. IX, 255 pp.
     29.2007, 47
     D. E. M.

329 [rev.] Li Jiubiao 李九標: Kouduo richao 口鐸日抄. Li Jiubiao's Diary of Oral Admonitions.
     A late Ming Christian journal translated, with introduction and notes by Erik Zürcher. Nettetal:
     Steyler Verlag 2007. 682 pp. (Monumenta serica monograph series 56.)  ISBN 978-3-8050-
     0543-2
     29.2007, 47–49
     D. E. M.

330 [rev.] Lars Peter Laamann: Christian heretics in late imperial China. Christian inculturation
     and state control, 1720–1850. London, New York: Routledge 2006. XV, 204 pp. ISBN 0-415-
     29779-0
     29.2007, 49–53
     Dominic Sachsenmaier, Duke University

331 [rev.] Yan Jiale 嚴嘉樂 (Karel Slaviček SJ): Zhongguo lai xin 中國來信 (1716–1735)
     [Letters from China, 1716–1735]. Lin Limei yi 林李梅譯. Zhengzhou 鄭州: Daxiang
     chubanshe 2002. 237 pp. ISBN 7-5347-2756-1
     Karel Slavíček SJ: Listy z Číny do vlasti (1716–1735). Translated and edited by Josef Kolmaš.
     Prague: Vyšehrad 1995. 269 pp. ISBN 80-7021-127-X
     29.2007, 54
     D. E. M.

332 [rev.] Nicolas Standaert & Ad Dudink, eds.: Forgive us our sins. Confession in late Ming and
     early Qing China. Nettetal: Steyler Verlag 2006. 268 pp. (Monumenta serica monograph
     series 55.) ISBN 978-3-8050-0540-1
     29.2007, 54–55
     D. E. M.

333 [rev.] Patrick Taveirne: Han-Mongol encounters and missionary endeavor. A history of
     Scheut in Ordos (Hetao) 1874–1911. Leuven: Leuven University Press 2004. 684 pp., 6 maps.,
     10 col. ill. (Leuven Chinese Studies 15.) ISBN 90-5867-365-0

29.2007, 55–56
D. E. M.


**30.2008**

334 In memoriam: Erik Zürcher 許理和 (1928–2008).
30.2008, 1–16
Adrian Dudink, Catholic University of Leuven
[With bibliography of publications on Christian subjects.]

335 The Acta Pekinensia project. By Paul Rule 魯保祿.
30.2008, 17–29

336 "The Ten Commandments" of João Soerio. By Gail King 歐凱妮, Brigham Young University.
30.2008, 30–55

337 [rev.] Jean-Pierre Charbonnier: Christians in China A.D. 600 to 2000. Translated by M. N. L.
Louve de Murville. San Francisco: Ignatius Press 2007. 605 pp. ISBN 978-0-898-70916-2
30.2008, 56–57
D. E. M.

338 [rev.] Claudia von Collani, Harald Holz, Konrad Wegmann: Uroffenbarung und Daoismus.
Jesuitische Missionshermeneutik des Daoismus. Berlin: Europäischer Universitätsverlag 2008.
144. (Daodejing-Forschungen 1.) ISBN 978-3-89966-263-4
30.2008, 57–60
D. E. M.

339 [rev.] Michele Fatica: Matteo Ripa e il Collegio dei Cinesi di Napoli (1682–1869). Percorso
documentario e iconografico. Catalogo della mostra. Università degli Studi di Napoli
"L'Orientale" e Archivio di Stato di Napoli. Napoli: Arti Grafiche Zaccaria 2006. 329 pp.
ISSN 1824-4181
30.2008, 60
D. E. M.

340 [rev.] Nicolas Standaert & Ad Dudink, eds.: Forgive us our sins. Confession in late Ming and
early Qing China. Nettetal: Steyler Verlag 2006. 268 pp. (Monumenta serica monograph
series 55.) ISBN 978-3-8050-0540-1
30.2008, 60–66
Jocelyn M. N. Marinescu, Kansas State University

341 [rev.] Peter Chen-main Wang 王成勉, ed.: Contextualization of Christianity in China. An
evaluation in modern perspective. Nettetal: Steyler Verlag 2007. 316 pp. (Collectanea Serica.)
ISBN 978-3-8050-0547-0
30.2008, 66–70
D. E. M.

342 [rev.] G. W. Leibniz: Die Briefwechsel mit den Jesuiten in China (1689–1714). Ed. & introd.
R. Widmaier; transl. M.-L. Babin. Hamburg: Felix Meiner 2006, CXXXVIII, 894 pp. ISBN
3-7873-1623-X

30.2008, 70–80
Daniel J. Cook, Professor emeritus of Philosophy, Brooklyn College, CUNY


**31.2009**

343 "Essay on the Term for Deity". A key text of William Jones Boone in his nineteenth-century
debate with Walter Medhurst on the Protestant Chinese term for God. By Thomas G. Oey
黃梅樹.
31.2009, 1–14

344 China im Lexikon für Theologie und Kirche (LThK) / Roman Malek SVD 馬雷凱.
31.2009, 15–55

345 The four editions of Couplet's biography of Madame Candida Xu. By Gail King 歐凱妮,
Brigham Young University.
31.2009, 56–63

Review article:
346 Visual culture as a historical source.
Marcia Reed and Paola Demattè, eds.: China on paper. European and Chinese works from the
late sixteenth to the early nineteenth century. Elisabetta Corsi, editorial consultant. Los
Angeles: Getty Research Institute 2007. X, 236 pp., 49 color and 68 b/w ills. ISBN 0-89236-
869-3
Nicolas Standaert: An illustrated life of Christ presented to the Chinese emperor. The history
of the *Jincheng shuxiang* (1640). Nettetal: Steyler Verlag 2007. 333 pp. (Monumenta serica
monograph series 59.) ISBN 978-3-8050-0548-7
31.2009, 64–67
D. E. M.

347 [rev.] Chen Min-sun: Mythistory in Sino-Western contacts. Jesuit missionaries and the pillars
of Chinese Catholic religion. Thunderbay, Ontario: Lakehead University 2003. 172 pp. ISBN
0-88663-045-2
31.2009, 68–69
Jocelyn M. N. Martinescu 倪卓熙, University of Toledo

348 [rev.] William Theodore de Bary, with contributions by Cheung Chan Fai and Kwan Tze-wan:
Confucian tradition and global education. The Tang Chun-I Lectures for 2005. New York:
Columbia Univ. Press 2007. 113 pp. ISBN 0-231-14120-3
31.2009, 70–74
Arthur Waldron 林霨 University of Pennsylvania

349 [rev.] Irene Eber: Chinese and Jews. Encounters between cultures 中國與猶太. London,
Portland, Or.: Vallentine-Mitchell 2008. XVII, 187 pp. ISBN 9788-0-85303-674-6
31.2009, 74–77
D. E. M.

350 [rev.] Björn Löwendahl: Sino-Western relations. Conceptions of China, cultural influences
and the development of sinology disclosed in Western printed books 1477–1877. [Cong
xiwen yinben shuji kan zhongxi guanxi. Zhonguo guan, wenhua yingiang he Hanxue fazhan]

從西文印本書籍看中西關係。中國觀，文化影響和漢學發展. The catalogue of the Löwendahl-von der Burg Collection. Forward by Han Qi 韓琦. Hua Hin: Elephant Press 2008. XLIX, 265; 374 pp. ISBN 978-974-9898-34-5
31.2009, 78
D. E. M.

351 [rev.] Luís Saraiva & Catherine Jami, eds.: The Jesuits, the Padroado and East Asian science (1552–1773). Singapore: World Scientific Publ. 2008. XX, 229 pp. ISBN 978-981-277-125-4 (History of Mathematical Sciences: Portugal and East Asia 3.)
31.2009, 78–80
Florence C. Hsia, Department of History of Science, University of Wisconsin-Madison

352 [rev.] Nicolas Standaert 鐘鳴旦: The interweaving of rituals in the cultural exchange between China and Europe. Seattle: University of Washington Press 2008. VIII,328 pp. ISBN 978-0-295-98810-8
31.2009, 81–84
Jocelyn M. N. Marinescu, University of Toledo

353 [rev.] Tao Zhijian: Drawing the dragon. Western European reinvention of China. Bern: Peter Lang 2009. 223 pp. (Euro-Sinica 12.) ISBN 978-3-03911-812-0
31.2009, 84–87
D. E. M.

354 [rev.] Hartmut Walravens: Richard Wilhelm (1873–1930). Missionar in China und Vermittler chinesischen Geistesguts. Mit einem Beitrag von Thomas Zimmer. Nettetal: Steyler Verlag 2008. 316 pp. ISBN 978-3-8050-0553-1
31.2009, 87–88
D. E. M.

## 32.2010

355 Two sonnets for Fr. John Witek SJ – in memoriam.
32.2010, 1
Jonathan Chaves

356 Necrology: John W. Witek SJ 魏若望神父 (1933–2010).
32.2010, 2–17
Xiaoxin Wu 吳小新, Ricci Institute for Chinese-Western Cultural History, University of San Francisco

357 The legacy of Pasquale d'Elia SJ 德禮賢 (1890–1963), mission historian and Sinologist. / Roman Malek SVD 馬雷凱.
32.2010, 18–62

358 Tang christianity as perceived by Jesuit missionaries and Chinese converts in the seventeenth century. By Matteo Nicolini-Zani 馬明哲.
32.2010, 63–88

359 [rev.] Chronique du Toumet-Ortos. Looking through the lens of Joseph van Oost, missionary in Inner Mongolia (1915–1921) by Ann Heylen. Leuven: Leuven University Press 2004. 409 pp. (Leuven Chinese Studies 16.) ISBN 90-5867-418-5
32.2010, 89–91
Jocelyn M. N. Marinescu, Unversity of Toledo

360 [rev.] [Ouzhou suo cang Yongzheng Qianlong chao tianzhujiao wenxian huibian. Wu Min, Han Qi bianjiao.] 歐洲所藏雍正乾隆朝天主教文獻匯編 [Compilation of Christian literature from the Yongzheng and Qianlong eras in Europe]。吳旻韓琦編校. Shanghai: Shanghai renmin chubanshe 2007. 12, 291 pp. ISBN 978-7- 208-07613-6
32.2010, 92
D. E. M.

**33.2011**

361 The Chinese Christian texts in the Zikawei 徐家匯 Collection in Shanghai; a preliminary and partial list / Adrian Dudink 杜鼎克.
33.2011, 1–41

362 Matteo Ricci's friendship with Qu Taisu 瞿太素. A key to the fate of the Jesuit China mission / Liu Yu 劉豫.
33.2011, 42–61

363 A translation of the journal (1749–1750) of Lucas Augustinus Ly (Li Shiyin 李世音, Chinese Catholic priest). Translated by Joseph Ruellen MEP. Annotated by Robert Entenmann.
33.2011, 62–77

364 [rev.] Ancestors, virgins and friars. Christianity as a local religion in late imperial China, by Eugenio Menegon. Cambridge, Mass., London: Harvard University Asia Center for the Harvard-Yenching Institute 2009. XX,450 pp. ISBN 978-0-674-03596-6
33.2011, 77–80
Henrietta Harrison 沈艾娣, Harvard University

365 [rev.] The birth of Orientalism. By Urs App. Philadelphia: University of Pennsylvania Press 2010. XVIII, 550 pp. ISBN 978-0-8122-4261-4
German Orientalism in the Age of Empire. Religion, race and scholarship. By Suzanne L. Marchand. Cambridge University Press 2009. XXIV, 526 pp. ISBN 978-0-521-51849-9
33.2011, 80–84
Francis X. Clooney SJ. Harvard University

366 [rev.] Handbook of Christianity. Vol. 2: 1800-present. Edited by R. G. Tiedemann. Leiden: Brill 2010. XLI,1050 pp. (Handbook of Oriental Studies, Section 4 China, 15.) ISBN 978-90-04-11430-2
33.2011, 85–87
D. E. M.

367 [rev.] A Jesuit in the Forbidden City, 1552–1610, by R. Po-chia Hsia. New York: Oxford University Press 2010. XIV, 359 pp., 10 color pl., 7 maps. ISBN 978-0-19-2010930311
33.2011, 87–89

Jocelyn M. N. Marinescu, University of Toledo

368 [rev.] Sojourners in a strange land: Jesuits & their scientific missions in late imperial China. By Florence C. Hsia. Chicago: University of Chicago Press 2010. XV, 273 pp. ISBN 978-0-226-35559-7
33.2011, 89–92
Joanna Waley-Cohen 衛周安, New York University


**34.2012**

369 The early Qing geographical surveys (1708–1716) as a case of collaboration between the Jesuits and the Kangxi court / Mario Cams 康言, University of Leuven.
34.2012, 1–20

370 The Kangxi emperor, Charles-Thomas Maillard de Tournon and Matteo Ricci / Claudia von Collani.
34.2012, 21–44

371 A translation of the journal of Lucas Augustinus Ly (Li Shiyin 李世音, Chinese Catholic priest). Part II: 1750–1751. Translated by Joseph Ruellen MEP. Annotated by Robert Entenmann.
34.2012, 45–58

372 [rev.] A new history of Christianity in China. By Daniel H. Bays. Malden, Mass.: Wiley-Blackwell 2012. X, 241 pp. ISBN 978-1-4051-5954-8
34.2012, 59–61
D. E. M.

373 [rev.] China's saints. Catholic martyrdom during the Qing. By Anthony E. Clark. Bethlehem, PA: Lehigh University Press, Lantham, MD: Rowman & Littlefield 2011. XIII, 277 pp. ISBN 978-1-61146-017-9 (Studies in Missionaries and Christianity in China, Pennsylvania State University.)
34.2012, 61–66
Jocelyn M. N. Marinescu, University of Toledo

374 [rev.] The Chinese roots of linear algebra. By Roger Hart. Baltimore: The Johns Hopkins University Press 2011. XIII, 286 pp. ISBN 978-0-8018-9755-9
34.2012, 66–69
Catherine Jami 詹嘉零
Centre National de la Recherche Scientifique, Paris

375 [rev.] The Emperor's new mathematics. Western learning and imperial authority during the Kangxi reign (1662–1722). By Catherine Jami. Oxford: Oxford University Press 2012. XV, 436 pp. ISBN 978-0-19-060140-0
34.2012, 70–81
Joseph W. Dauben 道本周 Department of History, Herbert H. Lehman College, CUNY & The Graduate Center, CUNY

376 [rev.] Im Spannungsfeld von Mission und Politik. Johann Baptist Anzer (1851–1903),
    Bischof von Süd-Shantung. By Karl Josef Rivinius SVD. Nettetal: Steyler Verlag 2010. XIV,
    971 pp. ISBN 978-3-8050-0569-2
    34.2012, 81–85
    D. E. M.

377 [rev.] A Jesuit garden in Beijing and early modern Chinese culture. By Hui Zou. West
    Lafayette, IN: Purdue University Press 2011. III,190 pp. ISBN 978-1-55753-583-2
    34.2012, 85–88
    D. E. M.


**35.2013**

378 Two powers without cannons, the late-Qing government and the Holy See / Luisa M.
    Paternicò, "Sapienza" University of Rome.
    35.2013, 1–16

379 Spaces for belief: Christianity, women and accommodation in seventeenth-century China /
    Gail King, Brigham Young University.
    35.2013, 17–34

380 The Zikawei 徐家匯 manuscript copy (1885) of Wang Zheng's Renhui yue 仁會約 (Rules of
    the Humanitarian Society)(1634) / Adrian Dudink.
    35.2013, 35–40

381 Biographical sketch of Herbert Allen Giles (1845–1935). By Phebe Xu Gray 徐秀麗.
    35.2013, 41–47

382 The discovery of Chinese Rites Controversy documents in a branch of the Bibliothèque
    nationale de France [Bibliothèque de l'Arsenal] / Mario Cams, University of Leuven.
    35.2013, 48–56

383 A translation of the journal of Lucas Augustinus Ly (Li Shiyin 李世音, Chinese Catholic
    priest). Part III: 1751–1752. Translated by Joseph Ruellen MEP. Annotated by Robert
    Entenmann.
    35.2013, 57–77

384 [rev.] Noël Golvers: Libraries of Western learning for China. Circulation of Western books
    between Europe and China in the Jesuit Mission (ca. 1650–ca. 1750). Vol. 1. Logistics of
    book acquisition and circulation. Leuven: Ferdinand Verbiest Institute 2012. 679 pp. (Leuven
    Chinese Studies 23.)  ISBN 978-90-8143-657-1
    35.2013, 78–80
    Jocelyn M. N. Marinescu, University of Toledo

385 [rev.] Noël Golvers: Portuguese books and their readers in the Jesuit mission of China (17th–
    18th centuries). Lisbon: Centro Cientifico e Cultural de Macau 2012. 296 pp., 12 color plates.
    ISBN 978-972-8586-25-6
    35.2013, 81–84
    Liam Matthew Brockey 柏理安, Department of History, Michigan State University

386 [rev.] Miroslav Kollár: Ein Leben im Konflikt. P. Franz Xaver Biallas SVD (1878–1936). Chinamissionar und Sinologe im Licht seiner Korrespondenz. Nettetal: Steyler Verlag 2011. VIII,910 pp. (Collectanea Serica.) ISBN 978-3-8050-0579-1
35.2013, 84–89
D. E. M.

387 [rev.] Negotiating religious gaps. The enterprise of translating Christian tracts by Protestant missionaries in nineteenth-century China. By John T. P. Lai. Sankt Augustin: Institut Monumenta Serica 2012. XIII, 382 pp. ISBN 978-3-8050-0597-5
35.2013, 89–93
Joseph Tse-Hei Lee 李榭熙, Department of History, Pace University in Manhattan, New York

388 [rev.] [Huabei di baoli konghuang. Yihetuanyundong di qian xi jidujiao chuan bo he shehui chongtu] 華北旳暴力和恐慌：義和團運動旳前夕基督教傳播和社會衝突 (Violence and fear in North China. Christian mission and social conflict on the eve on the Boxer Uprising) / 狄德滿 R. G. Tiedemann (author), 崔華焦 Cui Huajiao (translator). Nanjing: Jiangsu renmin chubanshe 2011. ISBN 978-7-214-07034-0
35.2013, 93–95
D. E. M.

389 Brief notices of publications in the field
35.2013, 95–96
[Shengjing di zhongwen fanyi] 聖經旳中文翻譯 (Biblical translation in Chinese).
[*Tianzhujiao yanjiu xuebao*] 天主教研究學報 Hong Kong Journal of Catholic Studies 2.2011. 564 pp. ISSN 2219-7664
China and maritime Europe 1500–1800. Trade, settlement, diplomacy and missions. Edited by John E. Wills Jr. New York: Cambridge University Press 2011. XIV, 297 pp. ISBN 978-0-521-17945-4
Light a candle. Encounters and friendship with China. Festschrift in honour of Angelo S. Lazzarotto PIME. Edited by Roman Malek SVD and Gianni Criveller PIME. Nettetal: Steyler Verlag 2010. 564 pp. ISBN 978-3-8050-0563-0
[Ming Qing zhi ji zhongxi wenhua jiaoliu shi - Mingji: qutong yu bianyi] 明清之際中西文化交流史 - 明季：趨同與辨異 (The history of Sino-Western cultural relations during the Ming-Qing transition – the end of the Ming: Convergence and divergence). By Shen Dingping 沈定平. Beijing: Shangwu yinshuguan 2012. 827 pp. ISBN 978-7-10008703-2

## 36.2014

390 Necrology: Björn Löwendahl 羅聞達 (1914–2013).
36.2014, 1–6
Sheila Markham, with contributions by Han Qi 韓琦

391 Wu Li's vision of zither music as resonating with christianity: Tones of Western wonders / Jonathan Chaves 齊咬翰, The George Washington University.
36.2014, 7–13

392 The Zikawei 徐家匯 manuscript copy (1885) of Wang Zheng's *Renhui yue* 仁會約 (Rules of the Humanitarian Society)(1634) [revised, with footnotes] / Adrian Dudink.
36.2014, 14–24

393 Old provenances of the Western books in the former (and current) Xujiahui (Zikawei)-library, Shanghai / N. Golvers 高華士, K.U. Leuven – F. Verbiest Institute.
36.2014, 25–42

394 Costanzo Varolio's *Anatomiae* as a source of [Johannes Schreck's] *Taixi renshen shuogai* 泰西人身說概 / Nicolas Standaert, University of Leuven.
36.2014, 43–58

395 A translation of the journal of Lucas Augustinus Ly (Li Shiyin 李世音, Chinese catholic priest). Part IV: 1753. Translated by Joseph Ruellen MEP. Annotated by Robert Entenmann.
36.2014, 59–70

396 [rev.] Giuliano Bertuccioli: La letteratura cinese. Revised edition, edited by Federica Casalin; foreword by Federico Masini. Roma: L'Asino d'Oro 2013. 473 pp. ISBN 978-88-6443-177-2
36.2014, 71–74
Marina Miranda 米玫香, Associate Professor, History of Contemporary China, Università di Roma "Sapienza"

397 [rev.] Wm. Theodore de Bary: The great civilized conversation: Education for a world community. New York: Columbia University Press 2013. 416 pp. ISBN 978-0-231-16276-0
36.2014,74–78
Ruth Hayhoe 許美德, Professor, Ontario Institute for Studies in Education, University of Toronto

398[rev.] Roger Hart: Imagined civilizations: China, the West and their first encounter. Baltimore: The Johns Hopkins University Press 2013. 374 pp. ISBN 978-1-4214-0606-0
36.2014, 79–81
Han Qi 韓琦

399 [rev.] Ines Eben v. Racknitz: Die Plünderung des Yuanming yuan. Imperiale Beutenahme im britisch-französischen Chinafeldzug von 1860. Stuttgart: Franz Steiner 2012. 328 pp. ISBN 978-3-515-10241-4
36.2014, 82–84
D. E. M.

400 [rev.] Nicholas Standaert: Chinese voices in the Rites Controversy. Travelling books, community networks, intercultural arguments. Rome: Institutum Historicum Societatis Iesu 2012. 473 pp. (Bibliotheca Instituti Historici SI 75.) ISBN 978-88-7041-375-5
36.2014, 84–87
Jocelyn M. N. Marinescu, University of Toledo

401 [rev.] Julia Stone: Chinese basket babies. A German missionary foundling home and the girls it raised (1850s–1914). Wiesbaden: Harrassowitz 2013. XXXIII, 237 pp. ISBN 978-3-447-06990-8
36.2014, 88–92
R. G. Tiedemann, Shandong University

402 [rev.] Ernest P. Young: Ecclesiastical colony. China's Catholic church and the French religious protectorate. Oxford: Oxford University Press 2013. XII, 383 pp.
36.2014, 92–96
Marianne Bastid-Bruguière


**37.2015**

403 Two Daoists who encountered Matteo Ricci in Nanjing: Xingshenzi 醒神子 and Li Chedu 李徹度 / Song Liming 宋黎明, Nanjing University.
37.2015, 1–11

404 The Lou-District Chinese Christian Orphanage, 1674–ca. 1850 / Gail King, Brigham Young University.
37.2015, 12–22

405 Dentrecolles's letters and the circulation of smallpox inoculation in the early 18th century as a Sino-Ottoman-European story / Wu Huyi 吳惠儀, Needham Research Institute.
37.2015, 23–41

406 Memoirs of Arne Benjamin Sovik 魏德光 (1918–2014).
37.2015, 42–69

407 [rev.] Anthony E. Clark: Heaven in conflict. Franciscans and the Boxer Uprising in Shanxi. Seattle, London: University of Washington Press 2015. XXI, 219 pp. ISBN 978-0-295-99400-0
37.2015, 70–73
R. G. Tiedemann, Shandong University

408 [rev.] Shu-Jyuan Deiwiks, Bernhard Führer & There Geulen, eds.: Europe meets China – China meets Europe. The beginnings of European-Chinese scientific exchange in the 17th century. Sankt Augustin: Institut Monumenta Serica 2014. VII, 224 pp. ISBN 978-3-8050-0621-7
37.2015, 73
D. E. M.

409 [rev.] Michael Kevak: Becoming yellow. A short history of racial thinking and race and racism in modern East Asia. Princeton: Princeton University Press 2011. 240 pp. ISBN 978-0-691-14031-5
Rotem Kowner & Walter Demel, eds.: Race and racism in modern East Asia: Western and Eastern constructions. Leiden: Brill 2012. ISBN 978-90-04-23741-4
37.2015, 74–84
Laura Hostetler 何樂娜, University of Illinois at Chicago

410 [rev.] Rotem Kowner: From white to yellow. The Japanese in European racial thought, 1300–1735. Montreal: McGill-Queen's University Press 2014. XXVIII,684 pp. (McGill-Queen's Studies in the History of Ideas.) ISBN 978-0-7735-4455-0
37.2015, 85
D. E. M.

411 [rev.] Michelle T. King: Between birth and death, female infanticide in nineteenth-century
    China. Stanford: Stanford University Press 2014. XIII, 250 pp. ISBN 978-0-8047-8598-3
    37.2015, 85–87
    Jocelyn M. N. Marinescu, University of Toledo

412 [rev.] Liam Matthew Brockey: The visitor. André Palmeiro and the Jesuits in Asia.
    Cambridge: Harvard/Belknap 2014. 528 pp. ISBN 978-0674-41668-0
    37.2015, 88–90
    Dominic Sachsenmaier, Georg-August University Göttingen

413 Addendum [to 36.2014, 14–24] Ad Dudink
    Corrigendum [to 36.2014, p. 60] Robert Entenmann
    37.2015, 91


**38.2016**


414  Dutch, Flemish and German engravings presented to the Kangxi Emperor. / Nicolas
    Standaert, University of Leuven.
    38.2016, 1–27

415 Was Xu Guangqi the author of the *Tie shizi zhu* 鐵十字著 (1627) which promotes the iron
    cross as a Christian relic? / Matteo Nicolini-Zani.
    38.2016, 28–42
    [With the Chinese text and translation.]

416 Jesuit correspondence from China: the two "Tartary-letters" of Ferdinand Verbiest SJ (1682
    & 1683) and their oldest printed edition (Paris 1684) as a case study / Noël Golvers, K.U.
    Leuven – F. Verbiest Institute.
    38.2016, 43–58

417 Der vergessene Castiglione-Experte George Robert Loehr und seine Briefe an Walter Fuchs /
    Hartmut Walravens 魏漢茂.
    38.2016, 59–73

    Review article:
418 Claudia von Collani, Erich Zettl, eds.: Johannes Schreck-Terrentius SJ. Wissenschaftler und
    China-Missionar (1576–1630). Stuttgart: Franz Steiner 2016. 446 pp.
    (Missionsgeschichtliches Archiv 22.) ISBN 978-3-515-11254-3
419 Shu-Jyuan Deiwiks, Bernhard Führer & Therese Geulen, eds.: Europe meets China – China
    meets Europe. The beginnings of European-Chinese scientific exchange in the 17th century.
    St. Augustin: Institut Monumenta Serica 2014. VII,224 pp. (Collectanea Serica.) ISBN 978-3-
    8050-0621-7
420 Isaia Iannaccone: L'ami de Galilée. Translated from the Italian edition L'amico di Galileo
    (2006) by Nathalie Bauer. Paris: Stock 2006.
421 Rainer-K. Langner: Kopernikus in der verbotenen Stadt: Wie der Jesuit Johannes Schreck das
    Wissen der Ketzer nach China brachte. Frankfurt a.M.: S. Fischer 2007. 313 pp. ISBN 978-3-
    10-043932-1
    38.2016, 74–81
    D. E. M.

422 [rev.] Noël Golvers: Libraries of Western learning for China. Circulation of Western books between Europe and China in the Jesuit Mission (ca. 1650–1750). Volume 3. Of books and readers. Leuven: Ferdinand Verbiest Institute, KU Leuven 2015. 637 pp. ISBN 978-90-8209-093-2
38.2016, 81–84
Jocelyn M. N. Marinescu, University of Toledo

423 [rev.] Paul R. Katz: Religion in China & its modern fate. Waltham, Mass.: Univ. Press of New England 2014. 264 pp. ISBN 9789-1-61168-543-5
38.2016, 84–87
D. E. M.

424 [rev.] Thierry Maynard: The Jesuit reading of Confucius. The first complete translation of the Lunyu (1687) published in the West. Leiden: Brill 2015. 640 pp. ISBN 978-90-04-28977-2
38.2016, 88–91
Wu Huiyi 吳惠儀, Needham Research Institute

## Index of Personal Names

As the name of the editor, often in the abbreviated form D. E. M., is mentioned in many records, it is left out here; only references to his *own* monographs are entered.

Abad, Antolin (OFM) 174, 203

Albrecht, Michael 45

Aleni, Giulio (SJ)(1582–1649) 126, 135a, 159, 213, 229

Alexandre, Egly 36

Anzer, Johann Baptist (1851–1903) (SVD) 376

App, Urs 365

Arelli, Francesco d' 197, 230, 287, 320

Babin, M.-L. 342

Bai Shangshu 白尚恕 31

Bailey, Gauvin Alexander 228

Baker, Donald L. 25, 35

Bastid-Bruguière, Marianne 402

Bauer, Nathalie 420

Bayer, T. S. [Gottlieb Siegfried] (1694–1738) 43

Bays, Daniel H. 216, 372

Bertuccioli, Bruno 246

Bertuccioli, Giuliano 伯佐良教授 (1923–2001) 116, 121, 195, 221, 246, 247, 277, 283, 396

Biallas, Franz Xaver (1878–1936) (SVD) 386

Bickley, Gillian 217

Bignon, Jean-Paul (1662–1743) 86

Billeter, Jean François 314

Blue, Gregory 257

Boone, William Jones 343

Bouvet, Joachim (1656–1730) (SJ) 51, 58, 69, 70, 86, 112, 249, 317

Boym, Michael (1612–1659)(SJ) 4, 76

Bridgman, Elijah Coleman (1801–1861) 192, 242

Brockey, Liam Matthew 柏理安 325, 385, 412

Buglio, Ludovico (1606–1682) (SJ) 200

Camps, Arnulf Pierre (OFM) 甘柏主教授 (1925–2006) 310

Cams, Mario 康言 369, 382

Camus, Yves (SJ) 210

Cardano, Girolamo 240

Carletti, Francesco 121

Carroll, John M. 326

Cartier, Michel 275

Casalin, Federica 396

Castiglione, Giuseppe (SJ)(1688–1766) (Lang Shining 郎世寧 ) 103

Caulfield, Caspar (CP)(†1993) 109, 130

Chan, Albert (SJ) 陳綸緒神父 (1915–2005) 251, 303

Charbonnier, Jean-Pierre 337

Chaves, Jonathan 齊皎翰 (1943–) 139, 228, 248, 271, 321, 322, 355, 391

Chen Cunfu 陳村富 169

Chen Min-sun 84, 107, 347

Chen Weiping 陳衛平 134

Cheung Chan Fai  348

Ching, Julia 秦家懿 [Qin Jiayi] (1934–2001) 132, 162, 291, 292

Cibot, Pierre Martial (SJ) (1727–1780)  127

Clark, Anthony E.  373, 407

Clooney, Francis X. (SJ)  365

Coblin, W. South  196, 319

Collani, Claudia von 柯蘭易 (1951–) 17, 51, 58, 69, 86, 112, 122, 138, 150, 153, 157, 161,
    162, 191, 193, 195, 249, 274, 317, 339, 370, 417

Cook, Daniel J. 173, 307

Corsi, Elisabetta  305, 346

Couplet, Philippe (SJ) (1623–1693) 55, 107, 166, 213

Covell, Ralph R.  62, 170

Criveller, Gianni (PIME)(1961–) 229, 389

Crouch, Archie R.  97

Cui Huajiao 崔華焦  388

Cummins, James Sylvester 53, 140, 270

Dauben, Joseph W. 道本周  375

De Bary, William Theodore (1919–2017) 268, 348, 397

Dehergne, Joseph (SJ) (1915–1990) 2, 89, 90, 276

Deiwiks, Shu-Jyuan  408, 419

Delahaye, Hubert 142

Demarchi, Franco  221, 283

Demattè, Paola (1962–) 346

Demel, Walter (1953–) 83, 133, 144, 409

Dentrecolles, François Xavier (SJ) (1664–1741) 405

Du Halde, J. B. (SJ) (1674–1743)  314

Dudink, Adrian 杜鼎克 113, 125, 137, 165, 185, 250, 289, 294, 309, 324, 327, 332, 334, 340,
    361, 380, 392, 413

Dunch, Ryan  252, 265

Eben v. Racknitz, Ines  399

Eber, Irene (1929–2019) 213, 349

Elia, Pasquale M. d' (SJ) 德禮賢 (1890–1963)  357

Elverfeldt-Ulm, Sigismund Frh. von  279

Engelfriet, Peter  257

Entenmann, Robert  149, 182, 201, 363, 371, 383, 395, 413

Etiemble, René  118

Faber, Ernst  239

Fang Hao 方豪 (1910–1980) 65, 312

Farmer, Edward L.  163

Fatica, Michele  202, 230, 339

Feith, Katharina  213

Feng Lan  316

Forte, Antonino (1940–2006) 121, 176, 277

Foss, Theodore Nicholas (1950–) 24, 37, 90, 237, 272

Fourmont, Etienne (1683–1745)  158, 281

Frémont, Christiane  117

Fuchs, Walter (1902–1979) 417

Führer, Bernhard  253, 408, 419

Gao Zhiyu  186

Gatta, Secondino  213

Gerbillon, Jean François (SJ)(1654–1707) 187

Gernet, Jacques (1921–2018) 114

Geulen, Therese 408, 419

Giles, Herbert Allen (1845–1935) 381

Girardot, Norman J. 296

Golvers, Noel 141, 231, 232, 278, 302, 384, 385, 393, 416, 422

Gonzalez de Mendoza, Juan 144

Goodrich, Anne Swann 98

Gray, Phebe Xu 徐秀麗 381

Grießler, Margareta 144

Grootaers, Willem A. 賀登崧 (1922–) 171

Gützlaff, Karl Friedrich August (1803–1851) 306

Han Qi 張星曜 224, 269, 325, 350, 360, 390, 398

Han, Gaspar (OFM) 174, 203

Hanan, Patrick (1927–2014) 254

Hao Zhenhua 鄗鎮華 54, 103

Harrison, Henrietta 沈艾娣 313, 364

Hart, Roger 374, 398

Hayford, Charles W. 199

Hayhoe, Ruth 許美德 106, 397

He Gaoji 何高濟 63

Henderson, John B. 179

Heylen, Ann 359

Heyndrickx, Jerome 107, 172

Holz, Harald 338

Hong Xiuquan 洪秀全 (1814–1864) 178

Hostetler, Laura 何樂娜 255, 285, 409

Hsia, Adrian (1938–2010) 夏瑞春 155, 244, 266

Hsia, Florence C. 351, 368

Hsia, Po-chia R. 367

Hu Kuo-chen Peter (SJ) 52

Huang Xiaojuan 黃曉鵑 328

Huang Yinong 黃一農 136, 185, 315

Iannaccone, Isaia (1950–) 116, 420

Isay, Gad C. 239

Jami, Catherine 詹嘉玲 142, 257, 351, 374, 375

Jensen, Lionel M. 113, 143, 220, 235

Jiang Shiquan 蔣士銓 321

Jiang Yonglin 163

Jullien, François 314

Kajdański, Edward (1925–) 76, 82

Kang Xiaolin 206

Katz, Paul R. 423

Kelsall, Ann Nottingham 15

Kern, Iso 131

Kevak, Michael 409

King, Gail 歐凱泥 166, 194, 218, 219, 226, 295, 297, 336, 345, 379, 404

King, Michelle T. 411

Kircher, Athanasius (1602–1680) (SJ) 77

Klaproth, Julius (1783–1835) 87

Klaue, Matthias 200

Klein, Thoralf 306

Kögler, Ignaz (1680–1746) (SJ) 300

Kollár, Miroslav (SVD) 386

Kolmaš, Josef (1933–) 177, 331

Kowner, Rotem 409, 410

Ku Wei-ying 古偉瀛 258

Kwan Tze-wan 348

Laamann, Lars Peter 330

Lach, Donald F. 143, 237

Lackner, Michael 61, 120

Lai, John T. P. 387

Laimbeckhoven, Gottfried (SJ)(1707–1787) 279

Lancashire, Douglas (1926–) 16, 52

Landry-Deron, Isabelle 314

Langner, Rainer-K. 421

Lazich, Michael C. 192, 242

Lazzarotto, Angelo S. (PIME) 389

Lee, Joseph Tse-Hei 李榭熙 387

Lee, Thomas H. C. 106, 115

Legge, James (1815–1895) 93, 104, 296

Leibniz, Gottfried Wilhelm (1646–1718) 86, 108, 117, 132, 138, 173, 225, 233, 241, 280,
   342

Leites, Edmund 8

Leslie, Donald Daniel (1922–) 213

Leung, Cécile 158, 281

Li Chedu 李徹度 403

Li Jianhua 李建華 313

Li Jiubiao 李九標 329

Li Lanqin 李蘭琴 92

Li Shen 李申 63

Li Shih-yü 李世瑜 [Li Shiyu] 171

Li Shiyin 李世音 363, 371, 383, 395

Li Tiangang 李天綱 215

Li Wenchao 李文潮 (1957–) 241, 256, 280

Lin Jinshui 林金水 41, 57, 111, 198

Lin Limei 林李梅 331

Lin Xiaoping 282

Lippiello, Tiziana 213

Liu Ning (Erzhi) 101

Liu Yu 劉豫 362

Lodwick, Kathleen L. 242

Loehr, George Robert (1892–1974) 417

Longobardi, Nicolo (SJ) (1565–1655) 157, 225, 280

Louve de Murville, M. N. L. 337

Löwendahl, Björn 羅聞達 (1914–2013) 350, 390

Lü Shijiang 呂實強 29, 30

Lubelli, Andrea Giovanni (SJ) (1611–1685) 309

Lundbæk, Knud (1912–1995) 1, 13, 19, 23, 39, 40, 43, 74, 79, 96, 101, 120, 127, 153

Lust, John (1918–2000) 88

Ly, Andreas 182

Ly, Lucas Augustinus (1719–1798) 363, 371, 383, 395

MacKerras, Colin (1939–) 259

Maillard de Tournon, Charles Thomas (1668–1710) 370

Malatesta, Edward J. (SJ)(1932–1998) 37, 52, 89, 186, 190

Malebranche, Nicolas 280

Malek, Roman (SVD) 馬雷凱 213, 260, 261, 262, 279, 284, 298, 312, 344, 357, 389

Marchand, Suzanne L. 365

Margiotti, Fortunato (OFM)(1913–1990) 129, 174

Marinescu, Jocelyn M. N. 倪卓熙 281, 311, 316, 340, 347, 352, 359, 367, 373, 384, 400, 411, 422

Markham, Sheila 390

Martini, Martino (1614–1661)(SJ) 19, 78, 150, 161, 221, 260, 283

Martzloff, Jean Claude (1943–2018) 7

Masini, Federico 195, 201, 246, 277, 396

Maynard, Thierry 424

Medhurst, Walter 343

Mei Wending 梅文鼎 (1633–1721) 7

Melis, Giorgio (†1990) 105

Menegon, Eugenio (1966–) 126, 148, 154, 159, 183, 211, 227, 285, 287, 364

Mir, Mark 303

Miranda, Marina 米玫香 246, 396

Moule, Arthur Christopher (1873–1957) 54

Müller, Andreas (1630?–1694) 82

Mungello, David E. 孟德衛 (1943–) 44, 73, 145, 175, 233

Naquin, Susan 167, 328

Navarrete, Domingo (1610–1689)(OP) 140

Ng, On-cho 220

Nicolini-Zani, Matteo 馬明哲 358, 415

Noll, Ray R. 146

Oey, Thomas G. 黃梅樹 343

Oh, Bonnie B. C. 84

Oost, Joseph van 359

Oxtoby, Willard G. 132, 162

Pagani, Catherine 285

Palmeiro, André (SJ) 412

Pantoja, Diego de Pang Diwo 龐迪我)(1571–1618)(SJ) 206

Paré, Ambroise (?1510–1590) 212

Paternicò, Luisa M. 378

Pelliot, Paul (1878–1945) 176

Perkins, Franklin 307

Pfister, Lauren 費樂仁 (1951–) 93, 104, 175

Porter, David 286

Poser, Hans 波塞爾 (1937–) , 256, 280

Pound, Ezra (1885–1972) 316

Prémare, Joseph de (SJ) (1666–1736) 120

Ptak, Roderich (1955–) 218

Ptolemy 240

Puhl, Stephan (1941–1997)  179

Qu Taisu 瞿太素 (1549–1612)  362

Raguin, Yves 甘易逢神父 (1912–1998) (SJ)  210

Rawlinson, Frank Joseph (1871–1937)  110

Rawlinson, John Lang  110

Reed, Marcia  346

Ricci, Matteo 利瑪竇 (SJ) (1552–1610)  16, 24, 32, 33, 35, 40, 52, 57, 137, 229, 250, 287, 362, 370

Rinaldi, Bianca Maria  293

Ripa, Matteo (1682–1745) 馬國賢  202, 207, 230, 339

Rivinius, Karl Josef (SVD) (1936–)  299, 376

Ronan, Charles E. (SJ)  84

Rosemont, Henry, Jr. (1934–2017)  173

Rosso, Antonio Sisto (OFM)(1904–1990)  128, 203

Rougemont, François de (SJ) (1624–1676)  232

Rouleau, Francis A. (SJ)(1900–1984)  37

Rudomina, Andrius (SJ) (1596–1631)  236

Ruellen, Joseph (MEP)  363, 371, 383, 395

Rule, Paul A. (1937–)  72, 335

Sachsenmaier, Dominic  189, 222, 263, 330, 412

Sadzevičiutė, Eglė  236

Sainte-Marie, Antoine de  280

Saraiva, Luís  288, 351

Schall von Bell, Johann Adam (Tang Ruowang 湯若望) (SJ) (1592–1666)  92, 119, 122, 213

Schreck, Johannes (1576–1630) (SJ)  394, 418, 421

Sebes, Joseph Schobert (SJ) (1915–1990)  91, 290

Shen Dingping 沈定平  68, 264, 389

Shen Fuwei 沈福偉  66

Slavíček, Karel (SJ) 嚴嘉樂 (1678–1735)  177

Smogulecki, Mikolaj (SJ) 穆尼閣 (1610–1656)  240

Soerio, João 蘇如望 (SJ)(1566–1607)  295, 336

Song Liming 宋黎明  403

Sovik, Arne Benjamin 魏德光 (1918–2014)  406

Spae, J. (1913–1989)  99

Spence, Jonathan 史景遷 (1936–)  96, 178, 214

Standaert, Nicolas 鐘鳴旦 (SJ)(1959–)  20, 42, 59, 85, 102, 113, 134, 164, 185, 209, 212, 240, 243, 289, 332, 340, 346, 352, 394, 400, 414

Stary, Giovanni (1946–)  156

Stewart, Frederick (1836–1889)  217

Stone, Julia  401

Struve, Lynn A.  219

Stücken, Christian  300

Sun Jiang 孫江  134

Sun Shangyang 孫尚楊  134

Sure, Donald F. St. (SJ)  146

Sweeten, Alan Richard  265

Takata Tokio  176, 205

Tamburello, Adolfo (1934–)  116

Tang Baisheng  206

Tao Zhijian 353

Taveirne, Patrick 301, 333

Taylor, Romeyn 163

Tiedemann, Rolf Gerhard 狄德滿 (1941–2019) 296, 366, 388, 400, 407

Tongrong (1593–1679) 131

Tucci, Giuseppe (1894–1984) 320

Uhalley, Stephan, Jr. 245

Van Hée, Louis (SJ) (1873–) 119

Van Kley, Edwin J. 范克雷 (1930–2002) 143, 272

Van Tuyl, Charles D. 77

Vande Walle, Willy F. (1949–) 302

Varo, Francisco 萬方濟各 (1627–1687) (OP) 319

Varolio, Costanzo (1543–1575) 394

Väth, Alfons (SJ) (1874–1937) 119

Verbiest, Ferdinand (SJ) (Nan Huairen)(1623–1688) 79, 111, 141, 179, 225, 278, 416

Wakeman, Frederic Evans, Jr. (1937–2006) 285

Waldron, Arthur 林霨 348

Waley-Cohen, Joanna 衛周安 (1952–) 235

Walf, Knut (1936–) 213

Walravens, Hartmut 魏漢茂 4, 21, 73, 87, 236, 354, 417

Waltner, Ann 163

Wan, Sze-kar 213

Wang Fu-shih 王輔世 [Wang Fushi] 171

Wang Meixiu 王美秀 204

Wang Qingyu 王慶余 47

Wang Tao 王韜 (1828–1897) 223

Wang Zheng 380, 392

Wang Zhongmin 王重民 64

Wang Zunzhong 王遵仲 63

Wang, Chen-main Peter 王成勉 341

Wegmann, Konrad (1932–2008) 338

Wesołowski, Zbigniew (SVD) 魏思齊 308

Widmaier, Rita (1942–) 108, 187, 225, 342

Wilhelm, Richard (1873–1930) 354

Willeke, Bernward Heinrich (OFM) (1913–1997) 128, 191

Wills, John E., jr. 140, 389

Witek, John W. 魏若望神父 (SJ) (1933–2010) 22, 91, 179, 286, 290, 355, 356

Wolff, Christian (1679–1754) 45, 132

Wu Huiyi 吳惠儀 405, 424

Wu Li 吳歷 (1632–1718) (SJ) 139, 282, 391

Wu Min 吳旻 325, 360

Wu Xiaoxin 吳小新 245, 318, 356

Wu, Lucio (1713–1763) 323

Wurth, Elmer P. (MM) 33

Xia Guiqi 夏瑰琦 184

Xingshenzi 醒神子 403

Xingyuan (1611–1662) 131

Xu Changshi 徐昌治 184

Xu Guangqi 徐光啓 (1562–1633) 64, 75, 257, 324
Xu Mingde 徐明德 78
Xu, Candida 徐甘弟大 (1607–1680) 166
Xue Fengzuo 240
Yang Guangxian 楊光先 (1597–1669) 136
Yang Tingyun 楊廷筠 (1562–1627) 85
Young, Ernest P. 402
Young, John Dragon 楊意龍 (1949–1996) 115, 145, 180, 181
Yu Shunxi (?–1621) 131
Yu, Anthony C. 139
Yuanwu (1566–1642) 131
Yves de Thomaz de Bossière (Mme) 187
Zeilinger, Gerhard 279
Zettl, Erich (1934–) 418
Zetzsche, Jost Oliver 234
Zhang Juzheng 張居正 (1525–1582) 13, 14
Zhang Kai 張鎧 206
Zhang Ruitu 張瑞圖 (1570–1641) 322
Zhang Xingyao 張星曜 224
Zhang Xuezhi 張學智 233
Zhixu (1599–1655) 131
Zhou Xianchen 137
Zhu Qingzuo 147
Zhu Weizheng 朱維錚 106, 180
Zhu Zongyuan (ca. 1616–1660) 222, 263
Zhuhong (1535–1615) 131
Zimmer, Thomas 354
Zingerle, Arnold 260
Zöllner, Reinard 306
Zou Hui 377
Zuloaga, I. (SJ) 32
Zürcher, Erik 許理和 (1928–2008) 113, 114, 329, 334

# Subject Index

R = review

300 Jahre *Novissima Sinica* 208
Academy of Sciences for China: proposal 86R
Acta Pekinensia project 335
Aleni, Giulio (1582–1649): biography 126, 213R
Aleni, Giulio: Poem in honour of. 322
*Anatomiae* (Varolius) 394
Anti-Christian opinions: China 29, 30
*Aomen jilüe* 澳門記略 40
Archives des Jésuites de Paris 2
Archives des Missions Étrangères de Paris – AMEP and their Chinese holdings 211
Archivo de la Provincia del Santo Rosario 148
Archivo Franciscano Ibero-Oriental (AFIO), Madrid (Spain) 154
Asia in the making of Europe 143R
*Astronomia europea* 141R
Astronomy: China 116R
Austria: Sinology 253R
Bayer, Gottlieb Siegfried (1694–1738): life and works 43R
Beitang Library: Chinese Christian books 294
Berlin: Chinese collections 5
Bertuccioli, Giuliano (1923–2001): Life and work 246, 247, 277R
Biallas, Franz Xaver: Life and work 386R
Bible in China 213R, 234R, 389R
Biblioteca Casatanense and its Chinese materials 227
Bouvet, Joachim: life and work 51R, 68, 69, 70, 86R, 112, 249
Bouvet, Joachim: Travels 317R
Boym, Michael: biography 76R
Bridgman, E. C: Sinology 192, 242R
Brussels: Royal Library: Chinese collection 327R
Buddha in China 59
*Budeyi bian* 不得已辯 (1665) 200R
Camps, Arnulf Pierre 甘柏主教授 (1925–2006): obituary 310
Castiglione, Giuseppe: battle pictures 103
Catalogue of Chinese and Manchu books: Academy of Sciences, St. Petersburg 87R
Catholic church: China: historiography 172R
Caulfield, Caspar (†1993): obituary 130
Chan, Albert 陳綸緒神父 (1915–2005): obituary 303
China 199R
China and Europe 60, 115R, 389R
China and the Netherlands 302R
China and the West 106R, 214R, 398R
*China illustrata* 23
*China illustrata*: translation 77R
China mission resources: Pennsylvania 46R
*China Mission Studies Directory* 6, 11
China mission: Italy: resources 197R

China: Catholic mission: archival material 297R
China: Christian orphanage 404
China: Christianity 265R, 285R, 328R, 330R, 337R, 341R, 364R, 366R, 372R, 379
China: clockwork 285R
China: ethnography and cartography 255R
China: European image of. 286R, 353R
China: flora 293
China: German foundling home 401R
China: history 235R
China: image 83
China: image in Europe 73R
China: image of Jesus Christ 284R, 298R
China: Jesuits 368R
China: Jesuits, after 1841 304
China: Jews 213R, 262R
China: literature 396R
China: mission 256R, 258R
China: missionary novels 254R
China: painting: perspective 305R
China: religion 423R
China: saints 373R
China: Western books 384R, 385R, 393, 422R
China: Western views 259R
China: Xu Guangqi 257R
Chinese and Jews 349R
Chinese characters, imaginary 23, 39
Chinese figurism 17, 58, 112, 127
Chinese influence on Englightenment 68
Chinese religions: Longobardi 157
Chinese Rites controversy 147R, 175R, 215R, 382, 400R
Chinese script: history 74R
Chinese-Western exchanges 318R
Chinese: phonetics 196R
Ching, Julia 秦家懿 [Qin Jiayi] (1934–2001): obituary 291
Christian charity in China 226
Christian mission: China 231R
Christian texts of the Yongzheng and Qianlong eras 360R
Christian tracts 387R
Christianity among minorities in China 170R
Christianity and modern culture 180R
Christianity: China 114R, 193, 204R, 216R, 243R, 245R
Christianity: China: resources 97R
Christians in China before the year 1550 54R
Christians: Hangzhou 145R
Cibot, Pierre Martial (1727–1780): life and work 127
Colloque international de sinologie 8, 36, 56, 94, 149, 275
Conference on the Encounter of Religions in China 81
Confession: China 332R, 340R
Confucian classic, translation 1
Confucian Reflection on the Enlightenment Mentality 189
Confucianism 220R, 348R

*Confucius Sinarum Philosophus* (1687) 1

Confucius: interpretation 72R

Convegno Internazionale Giulio Aleni 135a

Convegno internazionale su Martino Martini 19

Couplet Symposium at Leuven 55

Couplet, Philippe (1623–1693): life and works 107R, 213R

Critique of Christianity: China 131R

*Dace* 大測 (Schreck) 31

Daoismus: Jesuits 338R

Dehergne, Joseph (1903–1990): obituary 89

*Description de la Chine* (Du Halde) 314R

East – West exchange 134R

East Asia: mathematics 288R

East meets West: The Jesuits in China, 1582–1773 23, 84R

Education: China 397R

Elia, Pasquale M. d' 德禮賢 (1890–1963) 357

Enlightenment: China 132R, 162R

Europe and China 118R, 142R

Europe in China III 209

European astrology in China 240

European engravings for the Kangxi Emperor 414

European literature: image of China 244R

European-American Conference on Exchanges in East Asian Studies 80

European-Chinese scientific exchange 408R

Faber, Ernst: philosophy 239

First generation Christian converts 315R

*Flora sinensis* (1656) 4

Fourmont, Etienne: life and works 158, 281R

Franciscans and Boxer Uprising 407R

Franciscans in China 174R, 203R

French protectorate of the Catholic church 402R

Fujian-West: cultural relations 198R

Fuzhou protestants 252

Gerbillon, Jean-François (1654–1707): life and works 187R

Giles, Herbert Allen: biography 381

Glossary of the Mandarin language (Varo) 319R

Gospel in Chinese 62R

Gützlaff, Karl: life and work 306R

Hells: China 98R

History of Christianity in China project 95

Hong Kong: history 326R

Infanticide, female: China 411R

Infanticide: China 321

Institute for Chinese-Western Cultural History (San Francisco) 49

International Conference on the Life and Work of Ferdinand Verbiest 79

International Conference on Wang Tao and the Modern World 223

International Symposium "Giulio Aleni SJ (1582–1649), Missionary in China" 159

Italy and China 195R

Italy and the Orient 320R

J. A. Schall von Bell SJ, missionary of Cologne & astronomer of China. 122

Jesuit Archives, Rome: Chinese collection 251R

Jesuit catechisms  276R
Jesuit fiction  155
Jesuit mission  113R, 325R, 347R
Jesuit missions: art  228R
Jesuit tombstones  156, 167
Jesuit writings: China  42
Jesuits in China  102, 213R
Jesuits: Confucius  424R
Jesuits: East Asia  53R
Jesuits: image of Christ  229R
Jesuits: Sinology  44R
Jews in China  213R, 262R
*Jihe tongjie* (幾何通解  7
*Jincheng shuxiang* 進呈書像 (1640)  346R
Jinchuan War (1747–1749)  182
Jullien, François  314R
Kangxi Emperor and the mission  370
Kangxi Emperor: portrait  249
Kangxi emperor's edict of toleration  123
Kangxi: Jesuit atlas  369
Kögler, Ignaz: life and work  300R
Korea: Chinese Jesuit works  25
*Kouduo richao* 口鐸日抄  329R
Lach, Donald F. (1917–2000): obituary  237
Laimbeckhoven, Gottfried von: Letters from China  279R
Lazzarotto, Angelo: Festschrift  389R
Legge, James: biography  296R
Legge, James: works  93, 104
Leibniz and China  173R, 256R, 307R
Leibniz and Confucianism  233R
Leibniz-Archiv, Hannover  225
Leibniz, on Chinese Rites controversy  128
Leibniz: correspondence  108R, 342R
Leibniz: natural theology of the Chinese  280R
Leiden: Sinological Institute Library  20
*Lexikon für Theologie und Kirche*: China  344
Li Shiyin 李世音: Journal  363, 371, 383, 395, 413
Liu Ning (Erzhi) 劉凝 （二至）  101
Loehr, George Robert  417
Löwendahl-van der Burg Collection  350R
Löwendahl, Björn 羅聞達 (1914–2013): obituary  390
Lundbæk, Knud (1912–1995): obituary  153
Macau: history  218R, 261R
Malatesta, Edward J. (1932–1998): obituary  190
Manchu documents on Sino-Western relations  183
Margiotti, Fortunato (1913–1990): obituary  129
Martini, Martino: Collected works  221R, 283R
Martini, Martino (1614–1661): life and works  260R
Martini: tomb  78
Martino Martini and the China Mission of the Jesuits in the 17th century  161

Mathematics: China 374R, 375R

Mathematics: East Asia 288R, 351R

Matteo Ricci anniversary (Hong Kong) 33

Matteo Ricci quadricentennial celebration in the Philippines 32

Matteo Ricci's legacy in East Asia 35

Matteo Ripa. The Catholic mission in China (18th century) and the «Collegio de Cinesi» of Naples. 207

Melis, Giorgio (†1990): obituary 105

Ming history 163

Ming-Qing conflict 219R

*Monumenta Serica*: index 308R

*Monumenta Sinica* 290R

Müller, Andreas: manuscripts 82

Name of god: China 164R, 343

Naples: Collegium Sinicum 299R

Navarrete: Jesuits 140R

*Neue Welt-Bott* 274

Niedersächsische Staats- und Universitätsbibliothek Göttingen 26

North China: Mission 388R

*Novissima Sinica* 241R

Oost, Joseph van: missionary journals 359R

*Oratio de Sinarum philosophia practica* 45R

Ordos: mission 359R

Ordos: Scheut Mission 301R, 333R

Orientalism 365R

Palmeiro, André (SJ), in Asia 412R

Pantoja, Diego: 400th anniversary 206R

Paré, Ambroise: Anatomy 212

Passionists: China 109R

Perspective; painting: China 305R

Pineapple in China 4

Pound, Ezra, and Confucianism 316R

*Preliminary checklist of Christian and western material in Chinese in three major collections* 21

Prémare, Joseph de (1666–1736): life and works 120R

*Qinming chuan jiao yueshu* 欽命傳教約述 224

Race: East Asia 409R, 410R

Raguin, Yves (1912–1998): obituary 210

Rare books on China 346R

Rawlinson, Frank Joseph: biography 110R

Religion and culture 169R

*Renhui yue* 仁會約 380, 392, 413

Ricci and Daoism 403

Ricci and Qu Taisu 瞿太素 362

Ricci Institute for Chinese Studies, Taipei 50

Ricci, Matteo (1552–1610) 47, 57, 63

Ricci, Matteo: letters 287R

Ricci, Matteo: life and work 367R

Ricci's Church, in Beijing 194

Ripa, Matteo: and the Collegio dei Cinesi 230R, 339R

Ripa, Matteo: journals  202R

Rituals: China and Europe  352R

Roman Archives of the Society of Jesus: Christian texts  289R

Rosso, Antonio Sisto (1904–1990): obituary  128

Rougemont, François de: account book  232R

Rouleau, Francis A. (1900–1984): obituary  37

Rudomina, Andrius: life and work  236R

*Ruijianlu* 睿鑒錄  311

Schall von Bell, Johann Adam (1592–1666): biography  92, 119R, 213R

Schreck, Johannes (1576–1630)  418R–421R

Sebes, Joseph S. (1915–1990): obituary  91

Seduction of Chinese converts  238

Shanghai Library: Western rare books  147R

Shanxi bei jiaoqu dang'an  山西北教區檔案  313

*Shengchao poxieji* 聲朝破邪集  184R

*Shengjiao caicha ge* 聖教採茶歌  248

*Shixinlu xu* 始信錄序  136

Significance of the Chinese rites controversy in Sino-Western history  135

Simpósio internacional religião e cultura comemorativo Colégio Universitário de S. Paulo
    centenário  160

*Sino-Western Cultural Relations Journal*  267–271

Sino-Western relations 65, 66, 264R, 350R, 389R

Slaviček, Karel: letters from China 177R, 331R

Smallpox inoculation in China  405

Sovik, Arne Benjamin (1918–2014): Memoirs  406

Spae, J. (1913–1989): obituary  99

Stamps: Taiwan  34

Stewart, Frederick: biography  217R

Symposium on Martin Martini SJ and Cultural Exchanges between China and the West  150

Symposium on the History of Christianity in China  188

Taiping Heavenly Kingdom  178R

*Taixi renshen shuogai* 泰西人身說概 394

Tang Christianity as viewed by the Jesuits  358

Tartary, Letters from (Verbiest)  416

Ten Commandments (Soerio)  336

Theology, natural: China  117R, 280R

*Tianxue benyi* 天學本義  69, 70

*Tianxue chuangai* 天學傳概  18, 28

*Tianxue jijie* 天學集解  125

*Tianzhu jiaoyao* 天主教要  250

*Tianzhu shengjiao yueyan* 天主聖教約言  295

*Tianzhu shiyi* 天主實義  16, 52R, 137

*Tie shizi zhu* 鐵十字著 (1627)  415

Travels  121R

Travels in China  133R

Van Kley, Edwin J. (1930–2002)  272

Vatican and China  378

Vatican Library: Chinese collection  9, 176R, 205R

Verbiest, Ferdinand (1623–1688): life and works  111, 179R

Verbiest, Ferdinand: astronomical work  278R

*Wanmin simo tu* 萬民四末圖  309

Western books on China  88R

Western humanistic culture presented to China by Jesuit missionaries  201R

Wilhelm, Richard: life and works  354R

Willeke, Bernward H. (1913–1997): obituary  191

Witek, John W. 魏若望神父 (1933–2010): obituary  355, 356

Woodstock Theological Center Library  15

Wu Li: life and works  282R

Wu Li: poetry  139R

Wu, Lucio 吳露爵 (1713–1763)  323

*Xichao chongzheng ji: Xichao ding'an: wai sanzhong* 熙朝崇正集：熙朝定案：外三種  325R

*Xiguo jifa* 西國記法 61R

Xu Guangqi: tomb  324

Xu Guangqi: works  75R

Xu, Candida: biography  166, 345

Xuanhua: cultic buildings  171R

Yang Tingyun: biography  85R

Young, John Dragon (1949–1996): obituary  181

Yuanmingyuan 377R, 399R

Zhalan cemetery: Beijing  186R

Zhang Juzheng  13, 14

*Zhongguo Tianzhujiao shi renwu zhuan* 中國天主教史人物傳  312

Zhu Zongyuan  222, 263R

Zikawei Collection (Fujen)  165

Zikawei Library  48, 273

Zikawei Library: Chinese Christian texts  185R, 361

Zither music (Wu Li)  391

Zürcher, Erik 許理和 (1928–2008): obituary  334

Weitere Bücher desselben Verfassers im Verlag BoD

*Carl Graf von Klinckowstroem (1884–1969). Schriftenverzeichnis des Technikhistorikers, Wünschelrutenexperten, Okkultismuskritikers und Bibliophilen.*
Norderstedt: BoD 2015. 328 S.
ISBN 978-3.7386-3872-1

*Newspapers on the Mind – Around the World. The IFLA Round Table on Newspapers (RTN) 1989 – 2009.*
Norderstedt: BoD 2017. 296 S. 4°

*Julius Kurth (1870–1949): Briefe an den Dichter Börries von Münchhausen (1874–1945).*
Norderstedt: BoD 2017. 135 S.
ISBN 9783746030333

*Julius Kurth (1870–1949): „Autogramme" und Fabeln für Börries Frhr. von Münchhausen. Bibliophile Scherze.*
Norderstedt: BoD 2017. 99 S.
ISBN 9783746059976

(mit Christine Bell) *Mein inniggeliebter Louis!*
*Postkarten an den Elsässer Louis J. Stoffer (1889–1956), Hamburg und Tacoma*
*Ein Mosaiksteinchen zur Familien- und Auswanderungsgeschichte.*
Norderstedt: BoD 2018. 136 S. 4° (zweisprachig)
ISBN 978-3-7460-9487-8

Br. Berchmans Brückner SVD und die *Ars Sacra Pekinensis*. Briefwechsel mit dem Kunsthändler Walter Exner (1911–2003)
Norderstedt: BoD 2018. 166 S. ISBN 9783752820850

*Walther Heissig (1913–2005). Aus dem Nachlaß des Mongolisten und Ethnologen – Nachlaßübersicht – Briefwechsel mit Erich Haenisch, Lajos Ligeti, Käthe Uray-Köhalmi, John R. Krueger und Erik Haarh.*
Norderstedt: BoD 2018. 219 S. 4°
ISBN 9783748180708

*Statehood in the Altaic World.* Proceedings of the 59th Annual Meeting of the Permanent International Altaistic Conference (PIAC), Ardahan, Turkey, June 26–July 1, 2016.
Norderstedt 2018. ISBN 978-3-7528-0263-4

*Johann Redowskys Reise von Irkutsk nach Kamtschatka (1806–1807) im Auftrag der Akademie der Wissenschaften. Das wissenschaftliche Tagebuch des Forschers – Botanik – Geologie – Ethnographie der Jakuten und Tungusen*
Norderstedt: BoD 2019. 163 S.
ISBN 9783748188971

*George Robert Loehr jr. (1892–1974) und die Forschung über die Pekinger Jesuitenkünstler.*
Quellen und Materialien in deutscher Sprache
In Verbindung mit Marion Steinicke herausgegeben.
Norderstedt: BoD 2019. 489 S. ISBN 9783749410705
Walther Heissig: *Aus dem Nachlaß II:*

*Briefwechsel mit György Kara, Herbert Franke, György Hazai und Alice Sárközi sowie aus den Anfängen der Altaistenkonferenz (PIAC).* – Katalog mongolischer Blockdrucke in London.
Norderstedt: BoD 2019. 217 S. ISBN 9783739218830

*Zur klassischen poetischen Literatur Chinas. Leitfaden zu den Übersetzungen und Rezensionen von Erwin von Zach (1872–1942).*
Norderstedt: BoD 2019. 324 S. ISBN 9783741210174

*Neue Rückschau auf ein arbeitsreiches Leben. Hartmut Walravens zum 75sten: Thematisches annotiertes Schriftenverzeichnis.* Mit Einleitung und Registern.
Bibliographie – Bibliotheken – Zeitungen – Erotica – Normung – China – Japan –Altaistik – Mandschurei – Mongolei – Tibet – Rußland.
Norderstedt: BoD 2019. 236 S.  ISBN 9783748108610

*Verzeichnis der Veröffentlichungen von Professor Dr. Martin Gimm.*
Norderstedt: BoD 2020. 48 S. 4°
ISBN 978-3-7431-6665-3

*Franz Blei (1871–1942), Carl Georg von Maassen (1880–1940) und Hans von Müller (1875–1944) im Briefwechsel. Auch ein Mosaiksteinchen zur E. T. A. Hoffmann-Forschung.*
Norderstedt: BoD 2020. 168 S.
ISBN 978-3-7504-9525-8

*Jean Pierre Abel Rémusat (1788–1832). Zu Leben und Werk eines Wegbereiters der Ostasienwissenschaften.* Norderstedt: BoD 2020. 153 S.
ISBN 978-3-7519-3088-8

*Kleine Beiträge zur chinesischen Literatur- und Kulturgeschichte.* Mit einer bisher unveröffentlichten Würdigung des Geographen und Kartographen Albert Herrmann (1882–1945).
Norderstedt: BoD 2020. 196 S. 4°
ISBN 9783751944663

*Julius Klaproths (1783–1835) Briefe an den Orientalisten und Erfinder Paul Ludwig Schilling von Canstadt (1786–1837).* Samt Schreiben an den Sinologus Berolinensis sowie Ergänzungen zum Schriftenverzeichnis Klaproths.
Norderstedt: BoD 2020. 100 S.
ISBN 9783751984201

(mit Albert König) *Roter und gelber Papagei (Ara macao und Psittacula krameri, gelbe Mutation) am Kaiserhof in Peking.*
Norderstedt: BoD 2020. 44 S.
ISBN 9783752626445

Books on Demand (BoD)
In de Tarpen 42, 22848 Hamburg
Tel.: +49 (0)40 53 43 35 11
EMail: info@bod.de